Voices of unity

Essays in honour of
Willem Adolf Visser 't Hooft
on the occasion of his
80th birthday

edited by
Ans J. van der Bent

World Council of Churches, Geneva

The essays by Yves Congar and Alexandros Papaderos have been translated, from French and German respectively, by the Language Service of the World Council of Churches.

Second printing 1983

ISBN No. 2-8254-0664-3
© 1981 World Council of Churches,
150, route de Ferney, Geneva, Switzerland
Printed in Switzerland

Contents

Introduction

Philip A. Potter

It is always a joy to honour Willem Adolf Visser 't Hooft, especially now when he has attained the ripe biblical age of eighty. He has for sixty years been a clear, pertinent, and powerful voice for the unity of God's people so that they can together declare God's wonderful deeds and his purpose to unite all peoples and all things in Christ.

The "voices of unity" which speak in these essays must be seen as continuing a process of reflection on the ecumenical movement which Dr Visser 't Hooft has served with such unique distinction. They attempt to survey, in an informal and personal way, what has been happening in the ecumenical movement during the past fifteen years, and particularly since Dr Visser 't Hooft formally retired as the first General Secretary of the World Council of Churches. The contributors were asked to deal, from their different continental, cultural, and confessional contexts, with the following questions: "Where do you see contemporary history pressing upon the churches to act together? Where did the ecumenical movement *not* respond to the conflicts and pressures? Where do you see the Holy Spirit working in the church from your own continental and regional perspective?"

It is a particular pleasure for me to introduce this small offering to our beloved Wim Visser 't Hooft. It was my privilege to have a similar ecumenical background as his, having been active in the YMCA and the Student Christian Movement, and having served like him as Chairman of the World Student Christian Federation. I first met and heard him at my first world ecumenical encounter in 1947 at the Second World Christian Youth Conference in Oslo. It was he who encouraged me to speak at that conference and again on behalf of the youth participants at the First Assembly of the World Council of Churches in 1948. He invited me to join the staff of the Council in the Youth Department in 1954, and I learned a great deal from him during six years of close colleagueship. It was with this apprenticeship that I returned to the staff of the Council in 1967, just after he retired, as an Associate General Secretary, and since 1972 as General Secretary. It is an awe-inspiring experience to have shared with Dr Visser 't Hooft in being a voice of unity. He belonged to the second generation of the ecumenical movement, and I to the third generation. Those who write in this book span the second to the fourth generations of the movement. They have all, in different ways, been influenced by the witness of this great servant of the gospel.

Recently at the celebration of his eightieth year, Dr. Visser ' t Hooft shared with the Central Committee of the World Council of Churches his reflections on sixty years of the ecumenical movement.[1] He indicated that the early fathers of the movement sought to be "pan-Christians" concerned about the whole people of God, the universal dimension of the Christian faith, and the wholeness of the gospel. He went on to say: "It seems to me that these three emphases: the whole Church, the whole world, the whole gospel are not only an interesting part of our heritage, but abiding characteristics of the ecumenical movement. We would lose our identity if we neglected or repudiated them. And we need again and again to ask whether in our new and very different situation we are still the advocates and defenders of the biblical wholeness."[2] How are we being faithful to these abiding characteristics of the ecumenical movement? This is the question that the contributors to this book face in an engagingly open and honest manner and in terms of the last fifteen years.

The Whole Church

The significant fact of the last fifteen years is that all the major families of churches are now involved in the ecumenical movement. The year 1965 saw the end of the Second Vatican Council and the beginning of the Joint Working Group of the Roman Catholic Church and the World Council of Churches (which Dr Visser 't Hooft helped to create with Cardinal Bea). Father Yves Congar, an old friend and fellow pilgrim for unity of Dr Visser 't Hooft, who played an important role as a *peritus* at the Vatican Council, describes what this has meant for the Roman Catholic Church and for the ecumenical movement as a whole. It is all too easy to point to the difficulties that stand in the way of a breakthrough to visible unity between the Roman Catholic Church and the churches which gather together in membership in the WCC. What must be acknowledged is the extraordinary extent of the cooperation which has taken place in different parts of the world during this

---

1. "Pan-Christians Yesterday and Today," *Ecumenical Review*, XXXII, No. 4 (Oct. 1980), 387-95.
2. *Ibid.*, p. 391.

period. John Garrett and Roy Neehall speak of regional conferences of churches in the Pacific and the Caribbean in which Roman Catholics are active partners. José Miguez-Bonino describes how mutual hostility between Roman Catholics and Protestants in Latin America has been turned to a more open mutual recognition and conversation.

At the other end of the ecclesiological spectrum this has been the period when Pentecostal and Independent churches of Latin America and Africa have joined the ecumenical fellowship and have brought a breath of fresh air from the life and witness of people who have found new life in the Spirit. Mercy Oduyoye and José Miguez-Bonino remind us of this fact, which we have hardly digested in the ecumenical movement.

During these fifteen years there have been intensive discussions between world families of churches, and through the WCC Faith and Order Commission. Old issues which divided churches over centuries have been restated in ways which make them more susceptible to discussion and debate. On such central doctrines as Baptism, the Eucharist, and the Ministry theologians, at least, are reaching nearer to consensus.

The real challenge is that the ecumenical movement has seen ahead of the churches. We have not yet found the means by which churches can receive the insights gained in the ecumenical movement and thus can be enabled to venture forward in faith towards God's future for his people. It has been said that revolution, radical change, is a "long patience". I remember well Dr Visser 't Hooft telling us in the 1950s that it takes at least ten years for ideas emerging from the ecumenical pilgrimage to reach the churches. But patience demands strategies for change and relentless effort at all levels of the life of our churches. And this can only be done by committed groups, prepared to struggle with local congregations and also with the stubborn structures of the churches.

This point is powerfully stressed by that veteran ecumenical leader, M. M. Thomas, writing out of the Asian situation. Miguez-Bonino welcomes the painful process in Latin America of different ecumenical projects being given time to be related to each other by the churches' being in council with each other in each place. Congar pleads for a more eschatological approach, which is not an escape from obedience, but rather a constant turning to Christ, who has called us to be gathered under him as the one shepherd of the one flock in all our diversity. The task of bodies like the World Council of Churches, the regional conferences of churches, and national ecumenical councils is to provide the networks of contacts, communication, and fellowship by which God may do his own work with his people. In this I have always been guided by a remark I long ago heard Visser 't Hooft make: the churches have to be assisted to be unitable. This is the challenge we take up with greater determination in the coming years.

The Whole World

The last great event during the ecumenical leadership of Visser 't Hooft was the 1966 Geneva Conference on Church and Society. This was the first serious encounter between Christians from the rich North Atlantic and the poor South. Since then new opportunities and tensions have arisen among the churches. The first generation of ecumenical leaders thought that doctrine divided but that service would unite. They had a point, as Alexandros Papaderos demonstrates with regard to the Orthodox churches. It was through the expression of love in service that these churches came into living contact with the churches of the Reformation. But service can be narrowly conceived as the rich and powerful sharing the crumbs of their bounty with the poor. The 1966 Geneva Conference opened up a debate on the structures of economic, political, and racial injustice which has brought great strains to the ecumenical fellowship. While we are hammering out consensus statements on doctrine, the socio-political conflicts of our time, in which the churches are involved, are making evident the deep chasm which has long existed in the human family and which is reflected within and between the churches which participate in the structures of injustice.

Most of the essays stress this challenge of the whole world on the churches. My predecessor, Eugene Carson Blake, recalls his long and fruitful experience of the churches' attempt at coming to terms with the East-West ideological conflict. Since then there have been efforts at détente, and the role of the ecumenical movement in promoting détente has, in my experience, been a significant one, though it cannot yet be fully recounted. Alas, we are witnessing today an intensification of the East-West conflict, with the threat of a nuclear holocaust growing daily. The churches, as the people of God amidst the frightened peoples of the world, have an urgent task to be instruments of God's peace.

Alexandros Papaderos performs a fascinating service in his reflections on the conflict over the political commitments of the WCC, especially since he does so from an Eastern Orthodox perspective. He rightly affirms that if the WCC and the ecumenical movement are faithful to the gospel they are bound to be a necessary gadfly stinging the inert horse, as Plato wrote in his *Apology*. Emidio Campi similarly describes the agonizing struggle of students during these years to discern and witness to the gospel of God's kingdom and his justice. In my address to the Central Committee this year, which was itself a tribute to Visser 't Hooft, I emphasized the inevitable relationship between the churches' calling to unity and God's purpose to unite the broken human family:

> We will therefore not be bullied by those who attack us for giving our attention to controversial political issues either because they claim that it detracts from the proclamation of the Gospel and the search for the unity of the Church or because they do not wish to be involved out of fear or indifference or a feeling of helplessness. Necessity is laid upon us to witness to the Kingdom of God in these conflicts and to be instruments of God's reconciling work and act in Christ. In the midst of the gloom and despair of our time we must use every nerve of wit and will to let God's way be known and followed. In this we will join hands with all who are struggling for peace and justice in the world while we keep our minds firmly and critically centred in God's will and work. And in all this we will deploy what the German evangelist and social reformer, Christoph Blumhardt, called "the ceaseless prayer for the power of persistence", as those who fervently wait for the promise of the Kingdom.[3]

But when we speak today of the whole world we are also involved in the new enterprise of dialogue between cultures. For too long the unity of humankind was seen in terms of the ideologies of the North, whether capitalist or Communist. All over the world peoples are asserting and seeking to discover their own identity in relation to other peoples. The churches are part of this dialogue of cultures. Our ecumenical discussions on conciliarity, mission, and the dialogue with people of other faiths and ideologies have forced us to grapple with our divisions at a deeper level.

At the same time, most of us operate with a very parochial understanding of the world and of our churches. For most people Wesley's phrase "The world is my parish" would more correctly read "My parish is my world." Visser 't Hooft has warned that the just attempt at seeking cultural and national identities may make the churches forget that they are called to be the Body of Christ. But the Body can only function if the identity and contribution of its members are affirmed. This is the main burden of the essays in this book and it points to the immense task for the ecumenical movement in the coming years.

The Whole Gospel

The whole church and the whole world have their meaning in the whole gospel. That has been the basis of the ecumenical movement. When Visser 't

---

3. "A Growing Community of Faith," *Ecumenical Review*, XXXII, No. 4 (Oct. 1980), 385.

Hooft came into the leadership of the ecumenical movement in the 1930s and 1940s he had the advantage of knowing intimately and being able to interpret the biblical theological reflections of men like Barth, Brunner, Reinhold and Richard Niebuhr, John and Donald Baillie, Dodd, Maury, and Tillich — to name only the best known. Indeed, we of a later generation were formed by the unfolding of the whole gospel by these giants.

During the past fifteen years the conflicts and tensions of our world have forced Christians everywhere to go to the roots of their faith from within their own contexts. Out of this intense wrestling emerged a wide variety of expressions of the gospel. All the theologians mentioned above were from Western Europe and North America. Today, Latin Americans, black Americans, Africans, and Asians are doing theology out of the white heat of the struggle for the truth of the gospel in the midst of the travail of men and women for justice and for a truly human existence. The Eastern Orthodox, Pentecostalists, and Charismatics may seem far apart ecclesiologically, but they have one thing in common. They have brought to the fore a neglected dimension of the whole gospel — the person and work of the Holy Spirit and the spirituality without which there can be no living Body of Christ as a sign and sacrament of a truly functioning body politic.

One often hears criticism of the lack of theological reflection and evangelical zeal in the ecumenical movement. We would be nearer the truth if we admitted that we have been so imprisoned by our parochialisms that we have failed to listen to each other in order to discover together for our time the rich variety of the gospel being proclaimed. There are signs that we are opening ourselves to each other through opening ourselves afresh to God's Word. Here is indeed the heart of the matter. In this spirit I agree wholeheartedly with Visser 't Hooft when he writes:

> There is a future for the ecumenical movement provided it does not cease to reflect on its true *raison d'être*, and draws its life from the heart of the Gospel. Thus the movement will be moving forward. Then the Holy Spirit will work among the churches, taking us and our churches by the neck, driving and binding us together, and thus enabling us to carry out the renewing and saving task in the world.[4]

---

4. *Has the Ecumenical Movement a Future?* (Belfast, 1974), p. 97.

The World Council of Churches: East-West church relations 1966-1972

Eugene Carson Blake*

The subject of this essay in honour of my predecessor as General Secretary of the World Council of Churches is the development of East-West church relations, personal, political and theological. There is considerable comment on some events which occurred from 1954 to 1966, but these are chiefly incidents and occurrences in which I shared experiences with my predecessor or where what happened in the 1950s and early 1960s throws light on the events of 1966 to 1972. Properly here will be no analysis of events since 1972 when Philip Potter assumed office as the third General Secretary; he has the right and responsibility to comment on those years. Nor will this essay second-guess Dr Visser 't Hooft's guidance of the WCC from 1948 to 1966, much less his wide pre-Council ecumenical leadership during the late 1930s and the war years.

My first visit to the USSR was with an American church delegation in 1956. I was asked to go as President of the National Council of the Churches of Christ in the USA. It is important to remember that this visit came before the general programme of USA-USSR cultural exchanges began. Our American church constituency was unbelievably ignorant about the general culture of the USSR and knew even less about the churches under Stalin's regime. Our visit coincided with the end of Stalinism.

At this time of transition the leaders of the Russian Orthodox Church had begun to reconsider their 1948 decision not to join the World Council of Churches which was established that year. The large Eastern Orthodox churches of Georgia, Rumania, Bulgaria, Yugoslavia, and Poland had followed Russia's negative lead. But by 1956 Metropolitan Nicolay, as head of ecclesiastical foreign affairs for Patriarch Alexei, was leading the Russian churches to establish tentative relationships not only publicly with American churches but also quietly, as opportunity was found, with the World Council of Churches.

---

* Dr. EUGENE C. BLAKE was General Secretary of the World Council of Churches from 1966 to 1972.

During our 1956 visit in Moscow Franklin Fry, as Chairman of the WCC Central Committee, took opportunity to discuss privately WCC relationships with the Russian churches and particularly with the Russian Orthodox Church.

This earliest visit laid the foundations for my personal relations with Russian churchmen, which were important five year later in 1961 and ten years later in 1966. On that first trip I came to know not only Patriarch Alexei and Metropolitan Nicolay, but also Pimen, who was then abbott of the monastery at Zagorsk and is now His Holiness the Patriarch. I also met Buevsky, who was to become more and more important in relationship to the World Council as a lay member of the department of foreign affairs of the Russian Church.

The importance of this trip to the World Council of Churches stemmed from the unlikelihood that the Orthodox churches of Eastern Europe would become members of the WCC unless and until they had made some assessment of and adjustment to the churches of the United States, the nation which then and now seemed to them to be the chief political opponent of the Soviet Union.

On our first day in Moscow Metropolitan Nicolay invited our delegation to a private and informal meeting in preparation for the formal meeting to be held the next day, which would include representatives of almost all the churches in the USSR, Orthodox and Protestant.

It was a frank meeting and turned out to be useful. Metropolitan Nicolay made it clear that he believed he was talking to representatives of churches controlled by Wall Street. This did not surprise us, since we had become familiar with that attack on the American churches, printed regularly in the *Journal of the Moscow Patriarchate*. Rather than return the attack by accusing the Russian churches of being puppets of an atheistic Communist government (even though some of us at that time thought that they might very well be such), Henry K. Sherrill, then Presiding Bishop of the Episcopal Church in the United States, wisely chose to attack on the ground that the position of the Metropolitan and of his church was based upon lies about us and about the American scene. "You've got to tell the truth," said Bishop Sherrill that afternoon, not once but so many times that it finally got through to the Metropolitan that crude political propaganda was worse than useless in East-West church relations.

The formal meetings were less useful. Our hosts were not prepared immediately to question or discuss the formal presentations we made or to answer our questions directly. The pattern was rather a presentation from one side with perhaps a question or two for clarification, and a formal reply the next day from the other side. The subjects were not central or highly theological: I remember that we discussed the calendar (Eastern and Western), episcopacy, and race relations, among others. This was just as well, since only two or three of our delegates were really knowledgeable about the theology or ethos of the Eastern churches. The rest of us knew almost as little about the Russian Church and our hosts as they did about US Protestant churches and us. Henry Sherrill was one of our group who did know something about Orthodoxy. I recall his telling a young State Department aide who tried to brief us before our trip that he was talking nonsense about Orthodoxy and that he had been in and out of more Orthodox beards than the young man had ever *seen*. Paul Anderson, our interpreter, was the expert of our delegation not only in language, but also in Russian Orthodox theology and culture.

It was, all told, a successful visit and was followed by a return delegation to the USA in the spring of 1957. We made some friendships that last until this day. Dr Visser 't Hooft would be better able than I to assess how important the American initiative had been in clearing the obstacles to Russian churches' membership in the World Council, but the Russian Orthodox did join in 1961, and the others quickly followed their lead.

The political importance of this to the World Council of Churches was that it made it impossible any longer to characterize the WCC as a Western European and North American religious club. True, from 1948 there had been Eastern churches in the membership; but they were minority and Protestant churches, except for the Church of Greece and the Ecumenical Patriarchate of Istanbul; and politically and culturally both of these Orthodox churches were Western too.

During the next five years careful negotiations were carried on by Visser 't Hooft and the other officers of the Council. I had no direct part in these successful negotiations, leading to the application of the Russian Orthodox Church which came to the Third Assembly of the Council at New Delhi in 1961. The political complexity of relations with Eastern Europe was illustrated by the severe political strain under which relations with the two large Protestant churches in Hungary came during those five years when the Russian church was deciding to join.

In late summer 1956 the semi-annual meeting of the Executive Committee of the World Council of Churches was held for the first time in Eastern Europe, in the resort village of Galliatetto, Hungary. In November came the Hungarian uprising. Several weeks passed before it became clear what the Russian political and military response would be to a revolt which looked at first like a Yugoslavian type breakaway from USSR domination. During those several weeks of uncertainty the leaders of the three largest Hungarian churches — Roman Catholic (Cardinal Mindszenty), Reformed (Professor

L.Papp Lazlo), and Lutheran (Bishop L. Ordass) — committed themselves so far to the anti-Russian uprising that all were subsequently forced out of their ecclesiastical positions. Their churches then came under pressure from the government to repudiate them and their political actions.

But the churches were stubborn. When the World Council Executive Committee was meeting in January 1957 in Geneva, word came from J. Horváth, the Hungarian government's minister of church affairs, that he wanted to speak to Dr Visser 't Hooft about the continuing difficulties he was having with the member churches in Hungary. During the uprising he had been arrested and was in danger of being executed. His life was saved by the action of Bishop Ordass, who was unwilling that a good man, even though a Communist, should lose his life. But the people in the churches continued to be loyal to their old leadership and would not cooperate with the new ecclesiastical leaders being imposed on them by the government under direct Russian domination.

Dr Visser 't Hooft agreed to a meeting in Prague in a few days. It promised to be a difficult encounter since each of the partners in the dialogue had a different and conflicting agenda. The World Council General Secretary wanted to exert all possible outside pressure on the government of Hungary to save the lives and freedom of the Protestant bishops and other followers who had publicly supported them. On the other hand, Horváth wanted the World Council to put pressure on its member churches to cooperate with the government's department of religious affairs.

Visser 't Hooft decided he needed someone with him in Prague, since Czechoslovakia was hardly neutral ground, though the church situation then was much better than it was to be ten years later. He asked me to go with him, which I was glad to do. We flew from Geneva to Zurich, where we boarded the plane to Prague and soon found ourselves in the air with no embarrassing questions asked about our not having Czech visas. Needless to say, when we landed in Prague, we were detained by immigration authorities at the airport for several hours. We were able to get in touch with Josef Hromadka, distinguished theologian of the Church of the Czech Brethren and outstanding Protestant leader in Eastern Europe. He had some influence even on the Communist government of his nation. Hromadka came to the airport and succeeded in getting us through immigration, probably in part because of our date with the Hungarian government official, with whom they doubtless checked.

The conference next day lasted about seven hours and was a standoff. For our part we left uncertain about how safe our Hungarian friends would be, and on the other hand Horváth had to be satisfied with the knowledge that the WCC had no authority over its member churches and in this situation wouldn't try to influence them. In the next few years it turned out that the churches in Hungary did retain a measure of freedom, but the World Council of Churches had to settle down to working with church leaders who had been substituted for old friends (who were not martyred but were removed from regular contact with the centres of power).

At the WCC's New Delhi Assembly in 1961, the Russian Church made its formal application for membership. Their decision to apply had been known publicly for some months, and American church leaders had been bombarded with questions about whether a Russian church would actually be received. Some of us had stated flatly that they would of course be elected to membership if their papers of application were in order.

That was not the problem. The Russian Orthodox membership introduced into the life of the WCC an ethnic political tension among the Orthodox which had not existed until the "Rome of the North" appeared as a rival Orthodox influence to the "Rome of the East" (the Ecumenical Patriarchate at Istanbul). The latter had been the sole Orthodox voice in the World Council of Churches, representing not only Greek Orthodoxy but also exiled Russian and other anti-Communist émigré Orthodoxy in Western Europe and North America.

Even before the Assembly began there was trouble. On the Sunday before the opening sessions there was an Orthodox liturgy under the auspices of the Ecumenical Patriarchate, with Archbishop Iakovos celebrating. Normally in an Orthodox liturgy all bishops present and in good standing are invited to join in the celebration. Among the bishops present on this occasion was John Shavatskoy, Russian Archbishop of San Francisco, one of the leaders of an émigré Russian Church in schism with the Moscow Patriarchate. He was a member of an aristocratic Russian family, who had been in exile the forty-odd years since the Russian Revolution. Heading the new Moscow delegation was a very young Nicodim, who would later become Metropolitan of Leningrad and head of the department of foreign affairs of the Moscow Patriarchate. When it became clear to him that John Shavatskoy was participating in the liturgy, Nicodim arose and led the Moscow delegation out of the service!

That night I paid a visit to the hotel where all the Orthodox were staying. The atmosphere was explosive. Archbishop Iakovos was furious. He felt that the Russians, by walking out of the liturgy, had insulted not only him but also the Ecumenical Patriarch and God himself. I remember walking with him for ten or fifteen minutes up and down the spacious corridors of the hotel, letting him talk out his righteous anger and dismay. Later I paid a visit to the room of John Shavatskoy. Busy writing at a table, he said to me, "It is impossible for me to vote for the admission of the Moscow Patriarchate tomorrow, but I am trying to find the friendliest words I can use in a statement explaining my abstention." Culture and politics still remain more divisive among Orthodox and Protestants than does theology.

The next morning as I was sitting in the back of the assembly hall Visser 't Hooft asked me to come into his office near the platform. He had summoned Nicodim to a meeting before the session opened. When Nicodim came in, black-bearded, plump, less than 30 years old, it was my first meeting with one who became my closest Orthodox friend until he died of a heart attack in the very presence of Pope John Paul I in 1978. Like a Dutch schoolmaster, Visser 't Hooft dressed down the young prelate, who meekly listened. He made it clear that ecclesiastical insults could not be tolerated in the fellowship of the World Council of Churches. Then Nicodim replied. He apologized and said that it would not happen again. Nevertheless, he made it clear that he had had no choice but to leave a liturgy which included among the celebrants a Russian bishop who was in schism with Moscow. It was as good a performance on Nicodim's part as on Visser 't Hooft's. Both were principled and courageous. Both were basically friendly.

A few hours later the Russian Church was received into WCC membership by an overwhelming vote. At the Central Committee meeting which followed the Assembly, Nicodim was elected to the new Executive Committee.

In meetings of the Executive Committee during the next five years, I made it my business to listen to Nicodim very carefully. Gradually I learned to distinguish between Nicodim speaking for the record — that is, to be reported back home where he had to return — and Nicodim speaking to us really to persuade us to act in such a way that the Russian Church could live with it.

Let me illustrate the importance of this relationship with three incidents from the period later, when I carried the responsibility of General Secretary.

In January 1967 the Executive Committee met in Windsor, England, guests of Robin Woods, then Chaplain to the Queen. We were received warmly by Her Majesty and had a successful committee meeting. The press was clearly interested, especially in Nicodim, who consented to give a press conference in Fleet Street. Nicodim listened carefully as a Russian émigré revealed considerable knowledge of the church situation in Russia, reciting the number of churches that had been recently closed (the figure was in the thousands), the number of bishops and clergy imprisoned, and so on. When he had finished his devastating charges (all in the form of questions), Nicodim stood up to reply.

Though I made no notes at the time, I shall never forget his reply. "Let me remind you," he began, "that our church is situated in a nation which has only one party. That party is both Communist and atheist. The one party dominates the government nationally and locally. Now as to your questions: The number of churches closed during these years is not in fact as large as you say. You overstate the number. Furthermore, some churches have been recently reopened." Nicodim named some cities where this had happened. "As far as clergy being put in jail," he argued, "they were imprisoned because they had broken the law, preaching in the streets, organizing religious schools, and the like. Preaching by law has to be confined to the churches, and education is a state monopoly."

Then Nicodim concluded his statement as he had begun. "Our church survives in a nation which has one political party both Communist and atheist, and that one party dominates the government, nationally and locally." It was a virtuoso performance. Without telling a single untruth, Nicodim had made clear to those who would listen that, despite steady persecution, the Russian churches were surviving. Furthermore, he had said all the positive things he could that were true about Soviet government actions. The public effect was that he had blunted the émigré attack on his government.

My second illustration arises out of the Russian invasion of Czechoslovakia in the summer of 1968 at the very time of the Fourth Assembly in Uppsala. This was the first Assembly at which an adequate representation of Eastern Orthodox and Third World churches was present. The USSR had chosen this time to invade Czechoslovakia, until then the satellite country in Eastern Europe most free of religious persecution. The progressive government of Alexander Dubcek was quickly overthrown, and new pressures were put on all the churches.

The Church of the Czech Brethren communicated with me as General Secretary asking the World Council to take action critical of the Soviet invasion. I consulted with the newly elected chairman of the Central Committee, M. M. Thomas of India. We agreed that we could not act publicly at once. Since we were both roundly criticized later for the slowness of our action, I note here why we thought it better to delay. First, we knew enough not to trust the accuracy of the public press either inside or outside Czechoslovakia. In political matters, it is always necessary to have good channels of information. Furthermore, this was the first opportunity since the Amsterdam Assembly, twenty years earlier, to take a political stand that could not be discounted as simply a Western attack on the East. Now we were being asked to act by an authentic member church from the East. So M. M. Thomas and I sent telegrams to all the member churches in Eastern Europe, telling them of the Czech Brethren request and asking their advice as to what our reply should be. The Orthodox Church of Rumania promptly answered our telegram telling us to go ahead and protest the Soviet action. As I now remember it, we had no reply from Bulgaria; Hungary was definite against our acting at all. We had no official response from the German Democratic Republic, but word came quickly through the grapevine from Berlin that the church there hoped we would act. No word came from Nicodim.

Thomas and I waited no longer but released a brief, clear statement on behalf of the World Council of Churches, criticizing the Soviet Union for its invasion of Czechoslovakia. It was some weeks later that I heard from Nicodim through a mutual friend. His message was, "Tell Blake that if he must do things like that, to do them, but please don't ask us."

My third illustration has to do with the reconstituting of the Commission of the Churches on International Affairs (CCIA). The Uppsala Assembly had made it clear that the World Council of Churches could no longer function if it continued to be dominated by Western European and North American churches, especially in social, economic, and political affairs. The CCIA was now a department of the WCC. Its other parent, the International Missionary Council, had merged with the WCC at the New Delhi Assembly, and the constitution and by-laws of the CCIA had been redone by the Uppsala Assembly.

Since before 1948 the CCIA had done good work in international affairs at the UN, especially in the field of human rights. This was under the staff leadership of Frederick Nolde, a Lutheran theologian from the United States, Sir Kenneth Grubb, a layman of the Church of England, Dominique Micheli, who was Swiss Reformed, and Elfan Rees, a Welsh Congregationalist. This North Atlantic staff dominated the commission. Visser 't Hooft was also influential, as was commission member Connie Patijn, also Dutch. But this did not add up to an adequate international affairs instrument in 1968.

Soon after Uppsala it was clear that there would have to be changes in the staff. The director had had a heart attack and Sir Kenneth Grubb was at retirement age. As General Secretary, I had the task of proposing to the Executive Committee a new director. Following normal procedure, I first consulted the commission itself and the retiring staff, asking for suggestions and indicating my judgment that we should seek a director from some area other than the North Atlantic. I had little, if any, response — which indicated that my judgment was not shared by the old guard.

Months went by until I concluded that the best candidate I could find was Leopoldo Niilus, a lawyer from Buenos Aires. Getting good reports on him from South Americans and others who knew him, I formally presented his name to the commission. I do not recall any formal response from either the commission or the staff. Normally, in new staff appointments, the General Secretary made a recommendation to the Executive Committee, supported by the vote of the subcommittee or commission under which the new staff member would be working. Lacking such approval, I knew that I was facing a dangerous situation in recommending Niilus to the Executive Committee. Time passed. No other possible names were put forward. I decided to make the recommendation at the regular meeting of the Executive Committee being held in Tulsa, Oklahoma, early in 1969.

The atmosphere was fairly tense. Certain as I was that I ought to recommend Niilus, I did not want him or my recommendation turned down, as I feared it might be. Then in preparing the *curriculum vitae* for presentation, I suddenly became aware of another problem: though an Argentine who had received his secondary education in Sweden, Niilus had been born in Latvia and was thus a Latvian émigré from the USSR!

I hurriedly made an appointment to see Nicodim privately and explained my problem. I needed his support and his vote on the Executive Committee. I reminded him of my support through the years since 1961. I assured him that though Niilus was by birth a Latvian, and therefore an émigré, he was nevertheless not a Western European or North American in culture, mentality, or politics. He was an authentic representative of the Third World, which we needed. Happily, when I made my recommendation a few hours later, Nicodim came through with a motion that won over the doubtful votes. He proposed that we not take final action as an Executive Committee on such an important post, but appoint Niilus as recommended until the next meeting of the Central Committee, when they would act on the appointment. By the time the Central Committee met in Canterbury in August 1969 Niilus had done so well that he was elected without any negative votes.

Nicodim's trust and action were responsible for a very positive period in the World Council's influence on international affairs. Niilus with his new team of colleagues and the support of the General Secretariat had a great deal to do with new relations with Algeria, the making of peace in the Sudan after twenty years of war between the Muslim north and the pagan and Christian south, and avoiding with integrity taking one side in the Nigeria-Biafra war, in which there were clearly two sides, as the subsequent peace has shown.

Let me comment more briefly on the theological effect which the sharp increase of Orthodox churches and their representatives has had since the Uppsala Assembly. Perhaps the greatest immediate effect was psychological. The Orthodox no longer felt overwhelmed by Protestants and Anglicans, even though the smaller Protestant churches are necessarily over-represented, since a single representative cannot be divided in parts. But there was also a great psychological benefit to us in the West. There were now enough Orthodox speakers and thinkers in the committees and commissions to enable us to appreciate much more the richness and variety of the Eastern tradition.

I have never fancied myself as an academic theologian. But from university days I read enough philosophy and from seminary days enough theology to be satisfied that I can distinguish between sense and nonsense even in difficult theological speaking or writing. The greatest personal benefit which I have received from years of listening to the Orthodox is the lesson that biblical authority and tradition are not necessarily in conflict. From the Orthodox I learned in depth the evil and shame of schism in the one church of Jesus Christ. It was from contact with the Orthodox that I came to accept Calvin's sacramental theology rather than Luther's, Zwingli's, or Melanchthon's. It was from the Orthodox that I learned the weakness of the legalism of the Western church both Protestant and Catholic.

But I am still a Western Christian, closer theologically to Rome than to Constantinople or Moscow or Cilicia or Etchmiadzine. What I have been writing about is the mutual theological enrichment made possible and realized in the ecumenical movement since the full entrance of the Orthodox churches. The importance of this entrance was not diminished but enhanced by the new ecumenical stance taken by the Roman Catholic Church under the leadership of Pope John XXIII and Pope Paul VI. For the first time in a thousand years the whole Christian church began to be regularly together in friendship, discussion, and collaboration.

Every Western Christian, Protestant or Roman Catholic, needs to listen to and learn from the Eastern tradition and churches. We will be deeply enriched by the process. I believe that this enrichment will be mutual, though it is not for me to dwell on the potential gifts Western tradition, theology, and churches can offer the East. Due to the fellowship in the World Council of Churches, there are Orthodox theologians and ecclesiastical leaders who are in a position to write of this. Such Orthodox friends as Nikos Nissiotis and Vitaly Borovoy have done so and doubtless will do more. Only by such mutual enrichment can Christian unity, community, and communion come.

The ecumenical crucible:
a perspective on the World Student
Christian Federation

*Emidio Campi**

It is an honour and privilege for me to contribute to a festschrift for W.A. Visser 't Hooft, who served the World Student Christian Federation faithfully and intelligently as General Secretary (1932-38) and as Chairman (1938-49).

Since I am too involved in daily battles to write with sagacious intellectual serenity, this contribution is a more personal, even anxious, reflection about the present vocation of the WSCF. Of course, one cannot expect to arrive quickly at a clear understanding of this without confusion and uncertainty. Here it may be useful to have a quick look at the extraordinary story of the Federation (which was founded eighty-five years ago) to see what it might have to teach us for the present.

As both Ruth Rouse and Suzanne de Dietrich have amply documented, the WSCF's first fifty years were the most productive and dramatic in terms of the contribution that the WSCF made to the world church.[1] During these years, moreover, a relatively clear vision of the vocation of the Federation was embodied in two very distinct emphases:

(1) The Federation's role in the emergence and development of the modern missionary movement and of the subsequent formation and growth of the ecumenical movement. Any church historian would verify the strategic role the Federation has played in provoking and sponsoring key meetings and

---

* Dr. EMIDIO CAMPI has been General Secretary of the World Student Christian Federation since 1977.
1. R. Rouse, *The World Student's Christian Federation: A History of the First Thirty Years* (London, 1948); S. de Dietrich, *Cinquante ans d'histoire. La Fédération Universelle des Associations Chrétiennes d'Etudiants* (1895-1945) (Paris, 1948). See also H.R. Costou, Jr., "The World's Student Christian Federation as the Ecumenical Training Ground" (Northwestern University Ph.D. dissertation, 1963); H. O. A. Mayr, "Einheit und Botschaft." Das Oekumenische Prinzip in der Geschichte des Christlichen Studentenweltbundes, 1895-1937, mit einem Ausblick bis zur Gegenwart (Tübingen Ph.D. dissertation, 1975); C. Howard Hopkins, *John R. Mott, 1865-1955: A Biography* (Grand Rapids, 1979).

studies from which the thinking and programming that generated these two movements emerged. Leadership was nurtured and an initial testing ground for new visions was provided. Since the missionary and ecumenical movements constitute the two most important developments in modern church history, the Federation may be seen as one of the formative organizations of some of the key features of modern Christianity.

(2) The conviction — especially prominent in the minds of the early leaders — that students are a strategic point in the world. The special contribution of students is decisive in meeting the challenge the church faces in the modern world, and the Federation has been one of the primary vehicles through which the thinking, concerns, and needs of students and other members of the academic world have brought to the churches. At the same time, it has been one of the main media for enlisting students and young intellectuals in the task of bringing about the mission, unity, and renewal of the church. Thus, in this first period of its history the vocation of the Federation has never been limited to forming and upholding Christian student organizations, but has been understood more in terms of bringing university and church into dialogue with each other,

The years following World War II saw some vigorous rethinking of the vocation of the Federation. The foremost reason for this was the erosion of the clear but somewhat simplistic understanding of the mission of the church which undergirded the missionary enterprise. Dramatic changes in the world and in the life of the churches led to the end of the so-called "foreign missionary era" and called into question many earlier certainties about the relationship of the church to the world. Many assumptions about the role and function of the Student Christian Movements and the Federation were also brought under scrutiny.

Furthermore, the dramatic expansion of the work of the WCSF, from predominantly Western origins to a federation of movements in all the continents, posed new structural and ideological problems. The question of what unites the Federation in the midst of all the historical diversities which constituted its life became much more difficult to answer.

A third factor calling for rethinking was the formation of the World Council of Churches and the subsequent integration of the "missionary" and the "ecumenical" movements into one organization. What was now the task of the Federation within the wider ecumenical movement? Obviously the WCC had assumed many of its original concerns. The Federation responded to the new situation with two approaches. One basically continued earlier thrusts in new and exciting ways — the "Life and Mission" emphasis. The other stressed that the peculiar vocation of the Federation was to ensure a Christian presence in the university and in other institutions of higher education. This "university emphasis" began to show itself during the 1962 General Assembly at Nasrapur, India. By 1964, at the General Assembly in Embalse Rio Tercero, Argentina, it had become the central focus, and the final document of that Assembly, "Christian Presence in the Academic Community," marks the basic shift from a more general concern with the mission, unity, and renewal of the church to that of being the ecumenical expression of the ministry of the churches to a particular institution in society, the university.[2] Acknowledging this special role of the Federation, neither the World Council of Churches nor regional and national councils have created student departments.

The focus on the university as the locus for Christian presence was short-lived. Once more, events pushed the Federation to move further in rethinking its vocation for the present. Already in 1968, at the height of the student protests and the crises of the universities all over the world, questions began to be raised about the viability of the "university emphasis." No longer seen as a tool for bettering society, the university came to be considered as one of the institutions which perpetuate the prevailing structures of injustice and political oppression. Increasingly, the Federation began to assume a more political perspective. It began to concentrate on challenging both university and church about their role in the larger task of building a more just and humane society.[3]

Only in the light of this development can the preoccupations of the Federation since the General Assembly at Addis Ababa (1973) — when the theme "liberation" was adopted — be fully understood. In adopting this theme and clarifying it in Sri Lanka (1977) — "Christian Witness in the Struggle for Liberation" — the Federation emphasized its commitment to the struggle for liberation in its various forms around the world, and affirmed that, more than any other concept, "liberation" sums up the human aspirations of our time. It constitutes the primary historical challenge to which the Christian community as a whole must respond, in new and creative terms. Placing the Christian witness within the historical contradictions of today's world and proposing that in this context it must identify with the forces that seek to free peoples from conditions of oppression, the Federation redefined its vocation anew. As the latest statement of the "self-understanding of the WSCF" puts it, "the Federation understands itself as part of the Christian community and

---

2. V. Galand, "Christian Witness to the University," *Student World*, No. 4, 1964.
3. See the report and papers of the inter-regional consultation: "Towards a New Style of Christian Reflection" (Geneva, WSCF, 1970).

looks for new ways of expressing faith in the context of a political commitment to the struggles for economic, social and political liberation."[4]

Thus, over the last ten years or so the Federation has, on the basis of the gospel, explored untiringly how a just and peaceful society can be built and maintained. It has moved beyond general statements and now participates in the struggles for a new and just society. Whether addressing racism, sexism, the arms race and disarmament, or violation of human political, economic, social, and personal rights, Student Christian Movements have often been in the forefront. Not least important in the last few years is the way these movements and the Federation have been thinking afresh about education in a world riddled with threats to survival yet holding out the possibility of becoming a more just and sustainable society.

A sober assessment of these eighty-five years of thinking and working is bound to conclude that the Federation has not just moved but galloped. There have been a number of breakthroughs, which need not be set down here. But three points call for explicit mention.

First, in exploring how to be engaged more relevantly in the world, we have seen traditional sources of conflict literally vanish into the air. This is apparent in politics, for example. No longer can we draw a hard and fast line between Christian faith and the categories of Marxism — understood, now, not as a worldview but as scientific tools for interpreting society in order to change it. Being a believer and living out one's vocation in the context of struggles for human liberation are not incompatible. Without attributing messianic values to people's movements and without trumpeting "Christian solutions" to questions about building a new society, we have been involved in various struggles for the democratic transformation of society.

Second, the most important challenge facing humanity in this century — making the transition from nearly five hundred years of European domination to an era of mutual acceptance — led the Federation to try to rethink the relationship between member movements of the North and those of the South. This led to an act of great statesmanship — regionalization. In the simplest terms, regionalization was meant to reconcile the movements' demand for identity and self-determination with the fact that the world family must be built and upheld on foundations that allow for true expression by all. The aim of regionalization was to find a way of growing up into a mutual acceptance in freedom able to lead to a qualitatively new fellowship, unstable only because it is dynamic. Today, after twelve years of regionalization we

---

4. Minutes of the Executive Committee Meeting, Longueil, Canada, 1976; and of the General Assembly Meeting, Sri Lanka, 1977.

can say that this experience has had tremendous consequences and enables us and other organizations, however tentatively, to face divisions squarely and engage more truly in a covenant of common witness and service.

Third, and even more momentous, has been the growing realization of the need to take into account political, economic, and social factors when doing theology. The risk of calling things by their right names was fully accepted by the Federation. Materialist reading of the Bible, political theology, theology of liberation, the approaches of social psychology, and other more traditional theological methods, were widely and courageously used in the Federation.[5] Even in such thorny questions as the "materialist approach" to Scripture, it is possible to show that, in the context of a plurality of methods of biblical exegesis, this is a legitimate and indeed a challenging one.[6]

Over the years, we have found ourselves deeply divided on various political, theological, and organizational issues. It did not take long for some of the clarities of the early days to become clouded. As the Federation came to address social issues, the first split occurred, and in 1928 the Intervarsity Fellowship of Evanglical Students was formed. In the late 1960s, a paper called "Story of a Storm" attempted to describe the situation of the Federation as an irresoluble confrontation between those who want to evolve theology into Utopia and those who want to preserve the Christian tradition of the Federation. Clashing visions and actions have profoundly strained our fellowship, and yet there has been a great gain. The SCMs and the WSCF can no longer be described as ghettos or identified with the status quo. The stresses and strains have been worthwhile, for what we have gained during these crowded and eventful years represents an extraordinary rich endowment, which we are only starting to gauge fully.

Possibilities and limits in being a relevant Christian minority today

Of course, the WSCF is not the only movement in which Christians are earnestly seeking new ways of being relevantly engaged in the world for the sake of the gospel. I have seen the extraordinary wealth of experiences of many Christian groups, individuals, and institutions around the world. But these experiences are either historically short-lived or locally limited. They have not always come to terms with what we have been learning in the Federation. The WSCF does not represent a model nor a point of reference,

---

5. See E. Campi, "Notes for a Theological Balance Sheet of the 1968/1978 Student Generation," *WSCF Journal*, II (1979), 4-7.
6. See S. Rostagno, *Essays on the New Testament: A Materialist Approach* (Geneva, WSCF, 1975); D. Lochhead, *The Liberation of the Bible* (Toronto, 1976); various authors, *Introduction à la lecture matérialiste de la Bible* (Geneva, 1978).

but the eighty-five years behind us do represent an invaluable itinerary for all who combine a concern for building a new society with a sense of the need for worship, spirituality, and responsibility for the renewal and the witness of the church. This must be soberly but firmly stated! To regard this as an out-pouring of organizational pride would be profoundly unjust. For WSCF is not an ambiguous name. It means John R. Mott, Ruth Rouse, Dietrich Bonhoeffer, Visser 't Hooft, Suzanne de Dietrich, K. H. Ting, Philippe Maury, Philip Potter, Eduardo Mondlane, Maurizio Lopez, Editio Della Torre, and all the other students around the world who are spending their lives for the sake of an incarnated witness of the gospel.

In the world of the 1980s, threatened by destructive development, churches are desperately in need of renewal, and youth and students are desperately alone and in need of help. We are a minority — and not even a powerful minority — here. But it is my deep conviction that we can speak a word which others cannot or do not want to or dare not yet say. In so doing we shall have, if God wills, the unique opportunity and responsibility to be a *relevant Christian minority*, a minority which takes on itself the task of witnessing the full gospel by word and deed to men and women seeking to be God's instruments, participating in his liberation of all persons and all things in hope for the final manifestation of the new heaven and the new earth.

In practice, the possibility of and responsibility for building a relevant Christian minority today means four things to which I should like to call attention briefly:

1) to understand clearly the changing reality around us;
2) to have a theological-practical conception of our work;
3) to make full use of our federal fellowship;
4) to rediscover the missionary dimension.

To understand clearly the changing reality around us

The great and sometimes sudden changes around us affect people in different ways. Among young people and students in particular, they can occasion deep-rooted feelings of anxiety and frustration. If ever there was a time for serious reflection and stocktaking on the state and future of the world community, it is now.

During the last decade, the prevailing search was for political solutions to the problems of humanity. Today this trust has given way to widespread disinterest in and distrust of politics. The prevailing search now is for personal identity. How do we explain this complex phenomenon? Why are progressive forces presently unsuccessful in rallying the new generations around them? These difficulties can be explained within the framework of the "crisis of Marxism" — the rivalry between USSR and China, the war between Communist countries in Southeast Asia, in the Horn of Africa, after the invasion of Afghanistan, and within the framework of "critical theory" (Marcuse and Habermas). But these possible explanations must not be turned into an attestation of impotence before the "objectivity of the system." When the search for personal identity does not touch only a restricted privileged minority but involves large masses, it would be foolish and counterproductive to limit ourselves to moralistic denunciations. But if one recognizes the present demands for emancipation and autonomy of persons as a political factor, how can we orient the search for identity towards a collective opposition to the structures and powers which make them objects?

The past year has been one in which ghosts have walked. The people of the world have been reminded of the old Cold War notion of "balance of fear," maintained by constant military build-ups and renewed assertion of military might. Enthusiasm for détente has vanished. The threat of a general holocaust looms over the world, and peace sounds like a grandfather's tale. There is no need to belabour this point; every reader can complete this picture of distress and despair by simply recalling case after case in his or her own country or region. I mention this because the WSCF has since its inception always made great efforts, despite frequent disappointments and standstills, to implant in the consciousness of each generation of students the objective of striving "for peace and justice among the nations" (Constitution, art. 2,5). The challenging questions to be raised today are: What must we do in order to demonstrate clearly the objectives of a movement like ours? How can we effectively help dispel the erroneous notion of "balance of fear?" How can we contribute to the replacement of the present thinking based on weaponry by an outlook oriented towards a comprehensive reordering of international priorities, which strives to achieve some justice, peace, and progress? To some extent initial responses to these questions can be found already in the ongoing activities, but more vision, farsightedness, and courage are required if this arduous road is to be covered.

Another challenge is related to a particular area of our work. An increasing number of movements and regional programmes are giving priority to educational issues. Of course, SCMs and WSCF have always been concerned with the role of education and the definition of comprehensive educational strategies in the process of democratic growth of the masses. But the many changes in the student world of the last few years call for specific forms of reflection and action, updating, and indeed elaboration of new concepts. This new focus on educational issues, while representing an effort of unprecedented complexity and difficulty, has opened another chapter in our work. It has enriched our constituency and helped the Federation to redefine its identity on a more solid basis. In fact, even the initial results of our work are attracting much attention from various organizations, churches, and supporting agencies, which are looking at the Federation and its member movements as specialized bodies for educational issues. This is, however, a beginning, not an end; and much more solid work needs to be done to maintain the momentum and to ensure that the enthusiasm will persist.

Last, but not least, how do we explain the renewal and resurgence of religious attitudes the world over? No matter how we look at it, whether from the point of view of "radical theology" or of "historic materialism," the current religious phenomena are traditionally classified as "alienating." Are these interpretations still reliable? How, then, do we rationalize what seems to be a rekindled interest in religion, often of a very conservative type? If the traditional theological and political categories do not clarify the reality sufficiently, what other indications are there for a critical/practical understanding of it?[7]

To have a theological-practical conception of our work

A relevant Christian minority needs a clear theological-practical conception of its work. Without it our movement would be like a ship without a rudder. The choices we make imply assumptions about the task of the Federation: one cannot even draw up a budget or overrule the Standing Orders without theologizing. We need a theological-practical conception of our work which helps us to bridge the gulf between our theory and our practice, a theological tool which lets us know what it is that makes the Federation move. How is our staying together and living together as members of the same fellowship theologically guided?

We also need a theology in the Federation in order to arrive at clear and common criteria for evaluating what it does and says. At present we are in the dangerous situation in which activities are often judged from a great variety of different standpoints, each of which represents a specific interest. Some are exclusively concerned with the practical service the Federation renders; others consider that nothing counts except meetings; some see no point in the existence of the Federation other than its work for international solidarity; some ask only whether it is producing worthy publications. Thus we are in danger of generating a

---

7. See M. Miegge, "The Ambiguities of Religion in the 1980s," *WSCF Journal*, II/III (1980).

number of unrelated operations without a commonly accepted strategy in which first things come first. Now it is impossible to arrive at clear criteria unless we work out a coherent conception of the total task of the Federation, and we cannot see that task as a whole until we succeed in answering the basic question about its vocation and about the implications of its existence for the life of the movements and the Christian community at large.

Dietrich Bonhoeffer wrote in 1932 that "there is as yet no theology of the ecumenical movement" (he was referring as well, if not particularly, to the Federation):

> Each time when the Christian community in history has arrived at a new understanding of its own nature, it has produced a theology which expressed that understanding adequately... If the ecumenical movement is based on a new understanding of the Christian community, it will produce a theology. If it does not succeed in doing so, this will mean that it is nothing else than a purely utilitarian organization.

What would Bonhoeffer say about the Federation today? Probably something like this: There has been a certain amount of progress in clarifying the nature of Christian witness in the world. A number of questions about the relationship of faith and political engagement have been answered. We know better than before that theology is not done only in Central Europe and then exported to the rest of the world, sometimes directly but usually filtered through and simplified by moving across the Channel to England or Scotland. Now the winds are blowing from a slightly different direction. Increasingly we are hearing the sounds of creative thoughts from Africa, Asia, Latin America, the Middle East, and North America. But all this does not yet mean that we have a theological conception of the meaning of our present federal fellowship.

This has been the great weakness of discussions of theology in the Federation in recent years. We rightly emphasized the need for a plurality of theological approaches, but we failed to discuss how they can best serve the main purpose of the Federation; for all of them are essential if they enable us to gain guidance in our staying together and living together. Theology is not so much an exhibition hall in which ideas are polished and presented, as a laboratory in which tools are sharpened in order to give adequate responses to life situations. I hope that this will be seriously done. If not, it would mean, as Bonhoeffer said, that we are not engaged in a common spiritual enterprise with common assumptions about its meaning (to build a relevant Christian community), but rather in a purely utilitarian effort of practical cooperation.

The basic issues for a theological-practical conception of the Federation are: What is the whole calling of the Federation? What is the nature of the relationship the movements and regions have together in the Federation? Is it a purely organizational relationship, or is it an expression of real unity in faith, witness, and service? If the latter, how do we live out the various aspects of the life of the Federation?

To make full use of our federal fellowship

The possibility of building a relevant minority will largely depend on our being aware of the need to practice and develop our federal fellowship. I have dwelt at some length on this in my reports to the Executive Committee. Three years of experience in office have convinced me that this point should be reasserted more than ever. We have never been just a coalition, a council, an alliance. The constituent members of the Federation are engaged in a covenant, a pact of common witness and service. They are committed to growing into mutual acceptance of one another in freedom and respect. This is clearly stated in Article 2 of our Constitution, which specifically speaks of the task of the Federation as bringing together the member movements "into fellowship with one another in mutual service." Of course, nobody has an idealistic understanding of what fellowship actually means. We are left in no doubt that fellowship is fragile, always in the process of coming-to-be. It is inherent in fellowship to fight together, repent together, grow together. No one is spared this process.

Over the last three years or so, we have consistently become involved in promoting this sense of fellowship in the Federation. Perhaps the most significant achievement of the search for federal fellowship is the attempt at establishing the Ecumenical Solidarity Fund and the Universal Day of Prayer for Students. But much more has been happening nationally, regionally, and interregionally which has opened the way to a new style of thinking and being which is a prerequisite to engaging in a covenant relationship.

To rediscover the "missionary" dimension

A relevant Christian minority is an open and sharing community. In a sense the problem of the Federation today is a problem of communication. We have difficulty sharing insights and experiences with others, entering into ever-widening and deeper relationships, and keeping constantly before other Christian student groups and churches the urgency and the primacy of the issues we regard as fundamental. Perhaps this is painting too pessimistic a picture of the situation, but there are too many sectors of the Christian community whom we have not confronted with all we have been learning in the Federation.

I feel strongly that we must face these issues head-on. An officer of the Federation posed them in an arresting manner last year when he urged the Executive Committee to move from a "survival-oriented" Federation to a "mission-oriented" one. I agree wholeheartedly — even though the word "mission" scares many of us because of its associations with Western colonialism and imperialism and expansionism.

As I understand it, mission is not to convert "unbelievers" to the church, but to answer the serious question, "Where is God?" And if God has chosen the cross on which to be identified as God, where else can mission point to God except the cross? Where acts of injustice and inhumanity are committed, God is there. When people suffer at the hands of the economically and politically powerful, God is there. When death occurs, God is there. All this tells us that the "mission" of a community of believers is to be the sign and symbol of this intense and powerful presence of God. To rediscover this sense of our "missionary" vocation as a Christian minority scattered around the world is surely crucial for all our plans and projects.

Instead of a conclusion

"Have you ever thrown a pebble into a pond of clear, still water? You must have. When the pebble touches the water, it causes a small ripple which quickly turns into many ever-widening circles on the surface of the water and wherever the circumference of any circle touches another, it creates another set of concentric circles." As I was preparing this paper I came across this image by the Christian Chinese theologian C.S. Song. It reflects fairly well the history of the Federation during its first eighty-five years. But it would be inaccurate if the Federation did not increasingly recognize in the pebble the person of Christ. God became man so that we might recognize him and be aware that we are really known and really loved by him. This is not a task which will ever be completed, but I hope it is also not a task which will ever be lost sight of. This is my innermost wish for the Federation today and in the years to come.

Trials and promises of ecumenism

Yves Congar*

Elements for a theological assessment

These few pages, written in friendship and gratitude for the man who brought the World Council of Churches into being, make no claim to present a chapter of the history of the last fifteen years, certainly not in the sense of a narrative of events. Rather these are free-ranging reflections, from the theological point of view, on the present situation. Their partial and even markedly personal character will, I trust, be excused. I am conscious of not having given due place to other aspects: mission, evangelization, development and liberation, joint action in the world. From a theologian, theology is going to get the lion's share....

An assessment of trials

Ecumenism is a movement. If it had reached its goal it would *ipso facto* have ceased. As one delves deeper, one can only ask whether organic unity is really possible. Does "one flock, one shepherd" mean a single visible organism under a human religious leader? Will organic unity ever be attained in history? Or is it rather eschatological? I am more and more inclined to the latter view. I know that this has been severely criticized, tagged as defeatism, as a betrayal of Jesus' high-priestly prayer, "Father, that they may be one." And so it would be if it were to lead us to do nothing, to sterilize efforts towards organic unity. But our conviction is that history, even the history of the secular world, tends to eschatology. Consequently, that idea does not make ecumenical endeavours or advances pointless, any more than it demobilizes energies directed towards social justice, peace, a better economic order, fraternity. We must reach out towards organic unity. Efforts to attain

---

* Father YVES CONGAR, a French Dominican priest, is one of the theologians who has done most to inspire and further in the Roman Catholic Church the quest for the unity of all Christians.

it remain our goal; and the advances we make to it are not in vain. Far from devaluating them, eschatology gives them meaning and demands them.

Defeatism could come from another source, namely weariness and discouragement. Much has been done, but what difference has it made? The millions of kilometers travelled for conferences, the millions of hours spent, the tons of paper. And all for what? In 1927 the Executive Committee of the General Synod of the Reformed Church in the USA observed, regarding the comments made by the various communions on the final report of the Lausanne Conference, that each had stood its ground and made its judgments by reference to its confessional texts, and that — apart from the mutual tolerance shown — the replies would have been exactly the same at the time of the Council of Trent or the Diet of Augsburg.[1] The gains of the ecumenical movement in the area of doctrine do not appear to have had any effective follow-up. This was noted in regard to the agreement on grace achieved in Edinburgh in 1937. Once the curtain has been lowered, everyone goes home and things seem to go on as before.

Nevertheless, theologians have done a lot of work. Doctrinal agreements, which are imperfect yet in themselves substantial approaches to unanimity, are now numerous, and they deal with topics that are by no means peripheral or secondary. But these have not really gone beyond the world of theologians. What effective impact have they had on the life of the churches? Some, to be sure — for instance, recognition of baptism, or pastoral care in mixed marriages. But what church authorities have taken official notice of these agreements? That they can do only by carefully modulating their approbation, by adopting the method — at which the Church of England excels — of showing great flexibility in recognizing just what possibilities lie between all and nothing.

The Week of Prayer for Christian Unity, which had been such a powerful means of reestablishing neighbourly relations, is losing impetus. Although it still has its moments, on the whole it languishes. As one American correctly (if harshly) observed, the celebration of it is rather like a couple marking the anniversary of their engagement year after year but never actually getting married. Does the prayer for unity which consists in actualizing Jesus' prayer in us still occupy the place it once did, thanks above all to Abbé Paul Couturier? True, we pray *together* much more often nowadays, but do we pray for unity?

In a way, ecumenism may be the victim of its own success. We have acknowledged that we are brothers. To a large extent, the priority has been

---

1. L. Hodgson, ed., *Convictions* (London, 1934), p. 220.

restored to being a *Christian*, to a reference to Jesus Christ, as opposed to confessional particularism (which however persists). Many people, for example, in so-called charismatic groups, experience a unity already attained on the plane of the spiritual realities by which the Christian lives: Holy Spirit, Jesus Christ, the peace and joy of the sons of God. Others find themselves united in joint action for justice, or against racialism or torture. They do things together and converse with one another; but it is like going to spend the weekend in a country cottage or with friends. Afterwards, one goes back home. They are still different families. So we are living in a state of peaceful coexistence, with sectors of cooperation. We are in danger of being satisfied with this and of perpetuating a division which has lost its polemical or cold war features.

At best — perhaps "best" is the wrong word — the result is what I have several times analyzed as a union of Christians without union of churches. With young people, this is taken for granted: it is already quite something that they believe in God, in Jesus Christ, and pray. The form of the church matters little, and it were to claim to be important they would be mistrustful and critical. Granted that Christianity involves community, that a church is needed: one should go where one finds the greatest degree of spiritual help. This sort of outlook might be frankly accepted. One might claim that Christian substance is sufficiently present in the great confessions, that theological differences have been sufficiently smoothed out, that we can do more things together here and now and proceed to full recognition of ministries, to intercelebrations, to a common Eucharist.[2] But does this not overestimate the degree or quality of agreement we have reached? Does it not require one to forget or misconstrue the Orthodox Church, which has the sometimes inconvenient role of preventing any facile ecumenical pragmatism?

History, which exhibits a succession of separations, goes on. At the very time when ecumenical grace is operating in so many lives, new divisions are being created. Sects are multiplying. Some of these are in Africa, sometimes centred on a charismatic individual. Who has not heard of the growth of Reverend Sun Myung Moon's Unification Church? Among the churches, too, splits are in fact occurring. The Catholic Church no longer presents a monolithic unity. Internal ecumenism is needed, and it is hardly any easier to achieve than the other kind. The progressives are not interested in theological ecumenism, or in ecumenism of institutions, or in spiritual ecumenism. The integrists among us can think of nothing but "going back." Their numbers

---

2. This is in effect what Hans Küng advocates, for example, in "Anfragen an die Reformation heute," *Reformatio*, XXVII (June 1978), 374-93.

and the radical character of their reactions are such as to restrain the pastors, whose responsibility it is, from taking certain steps. Our bishops nevertheless deserve admiration for the freedom and modest courage with which they have performed many significant acts of ecumenical brotherhood, despite criticism and opposition.

An assessment of promises

A major fact of the last fifteen years has been the full and active entry of the Roman Catholic Church into ecumenical inquiry and repentance. Even so religiously homogeneous and traditionally dogmatic a country as Spain has been converted to pluralism and the acceptance of Protestants as partners. Indeed, ecumenism does not centre on the Catholic Church. It is not the only church, nor was it the first: Archbishop Söderblom could, after several refusals to participate, use the words of Mark 14:54: "*Petrus vero sequebatur a longe*" — Peter followed at a distance. But when the Catholic Church, with Peter at its head, did join the ecumenical movement, it made a very substantial contribution. I hope it will be permissible for a son of the Catholic Church to consider things mainly from a Catholic point of view. Readers will, I trust, forgive me for a certain one-sidedness or even provincialism of outlook.

For centuries Christians, having no problems about their personal identity, had scarcely any relation with "others" except in order to bring them over to themselves. That is evident from the exchanges, so often polemical, first between Latins and Greeks, later, in the 16th and 17th centuries, between Catholics and Protestants. Firmly installed in their own form of church, people acknowledged nothing beyond it. They assessed others on the basis of what they had that was identical to or consonant with themselves — or in order to reduce them to themselves.

Since the late 13th and early 14th centuries the Catholic Church has had a practical ecclesiology, dominated by juridical concepts: society, complete society (that is the meaning of *perfecta*), an unequal, hierarchical society with a distinction by divine right between clergy and laity. Such a way of thinking is ahistorical. I believe that the change witnessed at the Second Vatican Council was made possible by the entry of the eschatological point of view and consequently of a sense of history. Many of its great documents begin by assigning the church to its place in God's plan in the economy of salvation, itself flowing from the intratrinitarian life of God.

As a consequence, the form taken by the church, holy though it be, no longer had the absolute, petrified, exclusive, and intolerant character it may have presented before. Though not despised or neglected or even valued less, its significance was now relative. Christianity was seen to be in history, and other forms it had received in history were recognized as positive in the very features by which they differed from our form. Recognized status was given to pluralism, which was an unmistakable fact. The church opened itself to dialogue, and therefore to the beneficial possibility of receiving from others.[3] W.A. Visser 't Hooft clearly perceived the importance for all this of the Declaration on Religious Freedom. Not for nothing was it to be the responsibility of the Secretariat for Unity. With it, the Catholic Church disengaged itself from the Middle Ages (whose intellectual and spiritual heritage it obviously cannot sacrifice). It abandoned to its past a theory of the two swords.

We have undertaken a critical scrutiny of our past, an unsparing review of the many steps taken, the claims and ideas which have continued to play their part in our disagreements and our inability to understand one another. History has been of much service to us in this. H.J. Marrou speaks of the "cathartic value" of history: a genuine and soundly critical knowledge of the past frees us from its burden, which weighs down our present.[4] From this its ecumenical significance flows. It has rightly been emphasized that the ecumenical process begins with the work of purification within each church. The *Unitatis redintegratio* decree gives pride of place to the renewal of the church, and speaks of the need for permanent reform (Art. 6). So general and radical has this movement been in Catholicism that it has sometimes taken the form of systematic self-accusation. That was the price that had to be paid for the necessary ecumenical penance.

In dialogue and contacts, which had in fact existed before the Council, but which as a result of it became more frequent and assumed a new quality, Catholics have discovered "the others" as Christians and as brothers, and vice versa. There is a Christian substance which each church, although it is a concrete realization of it and lives by it, does not exhaust. Had that not been plainly shown by the formulation (at the Montreal Faith and Order Conference, July 1963) of a distinction between Tradition (singular), as transmission of the gospel and of the mystery of Jesus Christ, and traditions (plural), as historical forms taken by that transmission in different centuries and different confessions? Regrettably, if I am not mistaken, these views subseqently exerted scarcely any influence. To my mind it is a weakness of the World Council of Churches (as well as one aspect of its richness!) that as conference follows conference, it passes from one theme to another without sufficient continuity in following up earlier contributions. This criticism is less applicable to Faith and Order, but does the work of this commission enter into

---

3. Cf. the Decree on Ecumenism, and *Gaudium et spes*, Arts. 40-44.
4. H.J. Marrou, *De la connnaissance historique* (Paris, 1954), pp. 273f.

the proceedings of the WCC as much as it should? Here I am speaking as a theologian, obviously on behalf of theology.[5]

This liberation from the burden of a past of opposition and polemics, this discovery of Christian reality in others precisely at the point at which we differ, has been vitally experienced by the Catholic Church in the last fifteen years in regard to the Reformation and in regard to Orthodoxy.

It is scarcely possible to approach the Reformation except by way of the Reformers. Admittedly, they had not had a very good name among Catholics — Luther in particular, and, after all, it was he who started the Reformation. Thanks to historians, above all to Joseph Lortz and his disciples (in France, Daniel Olivier), we know that it is impossible to do justice to Luther without seeing him as a religious man who sought to restore the absolute primacy of the gospel, which is faith in the promise that God makes to us in Jesus Christ to blot out our sins. Very appropriately, this theme of "the gospel" was chosen for the first years of dialogue with the Lutheran World Federation, which resulted in the Malta Report of 1972. Since all the Lutheran churches refer to the Augsburg Confession, the question has recently been raised whether the Roman Church might be able to do today what it did not do in 1530, that is, recognize the Augsburg Confession as an acceptable, if incomplete, expression of the common traditional faith. Several, including Cardinal Ratzinger, have said that it would be possible.

Probably the most methodical and fruitful dialogue between Lutherans and Catholics has been in the United States. Starting with the creed and baptism, then passing on to the eucharist and the ministry, they finally reached in 1974 perhaps the most difficult of the questions that divide us, the papacy.[6] That fact in itself is a sign of the times. The convergence that can be expressed is considerable. Of course, Lutherans, just as much as Orthodox or Anglicans, remain a long way from the dogma of 1870; but we Roman Catholics also acknowledge more clearly the enormous share history played in the passage from "Peter" to "papacy" and in the declaration of the universal jurisdiction and infallibility of the Roman magisterium along the quite narrowly limited lines set forth by Vatican I. In view of what history tells us, including the history of Vatican I, in view of the questions and con-

---

5. One could recall here the criticisms constantly exressed by Orthodox hierarchs; e.g. quite recently by Metropolitan Chrysostom Zaphiris of Peristerion, in *Episkepsis*, No. 225 (Feb. 1980), pp. 12-15.
6. This subject has been treated in numerous publications which I have followed in my Bulletins in the *Revue des Sciences philosophiques et théologiques*.

tributions of ecumenical dialogue, including that with the Orthodox, and finally in view of the ecclesiology of communion and collegiality renewed by Vatican II, I think that Vatican I will have to be the object of a "re-reception," which might just as well be called "reinterpretation." Such a process has been engaged in for other dogmas, for example that of "original sin" and even that of Chalcedon. In the latter case, the confession of faith recited together by Paul VI of Rome and Pope Shenouda III of Alexandria is a brilliant demonstration that a reformulation or re-reception can take up the substance of previous "dogma" in a new form acceptable to two traditions or two churches.

Since I do not intend this as a chronicle of events, I shall only mention in passing the mixed commissions in which the Roman Catholic Church has participated with the World Alliance of Reformed Churches, with the Anglican Communion, with the World Methodist Council, with the Pentecostals, and finally with the World Council of Churches. On the Catholic side bilateral dialogues are much appreciated, for they permit of clearer delimitation of terms and conclusions. The multilateral — indeed, omnidirectional — character of the World Council of Churches is inherent in its constitution. That is its responsibility, but it is a very heavy one, and the effects of worldwide openness are perceptible. The work of bilateral commissions is likely to remain more narrowly ecclesiastical, though in this area it achieves indisputable depth and precision; whereas the work of the World Council of Churches generally has a markedly worldwide missionary character, directed towards the problems of humanity.

We realize that some problems are created, from the point of view of the World Council of Churches, by the existence of a *Catholic* ecumenism addressed to so many partners. The problem here is not one of principles, since the World Council allows the churches complete freedom to seek and conclude unions between themselves. Nevertheless the worldwide character of the Roman Catholic Church (not that it is alone in being worldwide, but in being worldwide in the way it is, with such strength and with such a centre of authority) may raise the spectre of a parallel ecumenism. The difficulty is met by increasing the flow of information and communications. In reality nothing is done in the absence of others.

This is true at the top. It is also true at the grass-roots. Perhaps that is where things are changing and maturing slowly to the point that will lead one day to the question whether we still have any reasons for being divided. Pulpits are being exchanged. At conferences a paper will be presented by a member of one confession without any "parallel" presentation from another. If the Catholic Church were to reform itself more totally according to the gospel norm, what conclusion would have to be drawn from the strongly attested fact that the 16th-century Reformers had no intention of forming a new church but only of reforming the old?[7]

Obviously, our Protestant friends will say that we are still wide of the mark, and recent events have revived latent anxieties and hesitations. We are thinking here of the impression given by certain features of the pontificate of John Paul II: the Mariology of Father Kolb, the massive reaffirmation of certain ethical positions, the greater prominence given to the person of the pontiff, and the measures taken against theologians, particularly Hans Küng. W. Pannenberg, who had committed himself in favour of a world ministry of unity assigned forthwith to the bishop of Rome, asked himself whether he could go on.[8] I think the question of an expression and ministry of unity — that of a *"Petrusamt"* or *"Petrusdienst"* — is deeper than the fluctuations of the events of the moment. But I believe equally that "papacy" also raises questions for Catholics acquainted with history and aware of the difficulties urged by all other Christian communions.

Even, or above all, by the Orthodox! It is not surprising that the Roman Catholic Church turns with special preference to the East to the Orthodox Catholic Church. For a thousand years it has never ceased trying to reestablish full communion, several times thinking to have achieved it, but never succeeding. Certainly no efforts were spared, but did these comport with the way things really were? Basically, their aim was to bring the Eastern Christians to the positions of the Latin West, with the sole proviso that their rites would be respected or even protected. Even at Florence in 1439, where there was a serious debate, the "proceeds from the Father *by the Son*" was accepted only in the sense of "proceeds from the Father *and the Son* (as from a single principle)." Nor is the question of rites merely one of language, rubrics, and beard. The rite incorporates and carries with it a whole mode of approach to dogma, a deep religious sensibility, the spirit, poetic feeling, and symbolism of a people. And of course the rite of the Eastern churches needs no more to be guaranteed or protected by Rome than the Latin rite by Constantinople or Moscow.

Actually, the more one really knows the Christian East, the more one realizes that in relation to us everything is fundamentally the same, yet

---

7. Jean Courvoisier has recently dealt with this question, concluding that "the very *raison d'être* of the Reformed tradition is to have an expectant and therefore provisional character. Like the Israelites en route to the Promised Land, the Reformed churches exist in view of Christian catholicity, and not in order to constitute one or several separate churches." *De la Réforme au Protestantisme. Essai d'ecclésiologie réformée* (Paris, 1977).

8. *Herder Korrespondenz*, 1980, p. 59.

everything is different, even what is the same. I could illustrate this by trinitarian theology, the celebration of the sacraments, the meaning of the "magisterium," or the understanding of the religious life. The secret of an approach to union is to recognize and accept this. The Roman Catholic Church has begun to do so.

First an accumulation of reasons for complaint and mistrust had to be overcome. For fifteen years this has been the concern of the "dialogue of charity," for which the Catholic Church and the papacy have managed to pay the price. The pope took the first step and went to the East, to Jerusalem and Istanbul. His visits were returned. When Metropolitan Meliton of Chalcedon came to Rome on December 7, 1975, Paul VI went down on his knees to him and kissed his feet, which moved Patriarch Dimitrios to say, "Paul VI has gone ahead of the papacy." But Paul VI had on two occasions, during the course of the Council and then before the Cross of Jesus in Jerusalem, asked forgiveness from all our brothers for whatever harm our church may have done them. It had been ten years before, on the last day of the conciliar assembly, December 7, 1965, that the act by which the two churches annulled the anathemas they had pronounced against one another in 1054, had been read simultaneously in Istanbul and Rome. It was the equivalent of a catharsis, of liberation from the historical and sociological burden of the times of disagreements. The dialogue of charity was then accentuated by the solemn restitution to Orthodox or Coptic churches of major relics which had mostly been entrusted to Rome or to Venice at the time of the Turkish conquest. Above all there was the exchange of letters, telegrams, and speeches.[9]

On several occasions in these documents the Church of Rome and that of Constantinople refer to one another as sister churches. In the rather distant past, that was a more or less standard way of putting things. As an expression of new relations, however, it assumes an extremely strong meaning. How can Rome any longer speak of itself as "mother and mistress?" There can be an elder sister, but both have the same father; let us say that their apostolicity is equal. Theological discussions are about to begin between the Roman Catholic Church and the Orthodox. Such dialogue already exists between Orthodoxy and the Anglican Communion, the Evangelical Church in Germany, and the Union of Utrecht ("Old Catholics" or "Catholic Christians"). I view this as extremely important. Orthodoxy always has a profound contribution to make. In it, a very rich spiritual tradition is alive. The East,

---

9. Published in the *Tomos Agapis* (Vatican and Phanar, 1971).

which we have half forgotten, must once again be present and fruitful in our Christianity.

Sooner or later, these theological discussions will get to the question of the procession of the Holy Spirit. In the Moscow and Belgrade conferences (1966) with Anglicans and Old Catholics, the Orthodox demanded and obtained the suppression of the *Filioque* in the Creed. The Anglicans had difficulty in agreeing to this and only did so while maintaining the legitimacy of the doctrine, which has been unanimously held in the West since the 4th century, which was maintained by the Reformers, and which has been vigorously defended by Karl Barth. In fact this doctrine is necessary in the Latin approach to the mystery of the tri-unity of God. It is the necessary condition of a full affirmation of the consubstantiality of the Son with the Father and of the distinction between the two hypostases of the Son and the Spirit. It was professed in the West during the six centuries in which it was in communion with the East. The Greeks formulate differently their affirmation of the same fundamental faith. I have just given serious study to this question and to the two traditions for my third volume devoted to the Holy Spirit. My conviction is that we have to acknowledge the coexistence of the two traditions, each complete and consistent, but impossible to superimpose. We will have to recognize and accept that we are different if we are to recognize our radical unanimity.

This poses a serious question, since the *Filioque* is a dogma for us, not just a theologumenon. But the problem will also arise with respect to other articles. Theologians of the calibre of Louis Bouyer and Avery Dulles have responded to this issue by claiming that a restoration of full communion would be possible without either of the two churches obliging the other to hold all that it may have determined, and even defined, as dogma during the period of a break in communion which was in any case never a complete one.[10]

* * *

I think the prime theological problem raised by ecumenism today is that of specifying as far as possible what differences are compatible with the establishment of full communion. What diversity can authentic organic unity admit? For this reason I have chosen as the subject of the course I am giving this year at the Higher Institute of Ecumenical Studies of the Catholic Institute, Paris (ISEO) the problem of "reconciled diversity," as it has been

---

10. Cf. Bouyer in *Istina*, XIV (1969), 112-15; Dulles in *Theological Studies*, XXIX (1968), 393-416.

called by the tenth assembly of the Lutheran World Federation (Dar-es-Salaam, June 1977; the term was launched in 1974 by the Conference of the Secretaries of the World Confessional Families). Already in Lausanne in 1927 Nathan Söderblom spoke of *"Einheit in der Mannigfaltigkeit."* No doubt he did so in a different respect and a different theological context from mine. For my part I have begun a wide-ranging historical inquiry in the domain of facts, texts, and projects. We shall obviously encounter the concept of "fundamental articles" which is not the same as that of the "hierarchy of truths" of the conciliar decree on Ecumenism (Art.11). But as yet I do not know what my conclusions are going to be.

Can we not think that all Christian communions aim at the fullness of Christianity? That fullness resides in Jesus Christ and in the Holy Spirit whom he gives. Can we say that the various communions represent ways of relating themselves to that plenitude? Holy people attain it — in many cases, certainly, thanks to their church; but can it also perhaps be attained in spite of the church or beyond it? Are there wounds and loss of wholeness on the level of the churches *as such*? Tradition and history answer Yes. Of what kind?

Pastor Roger Mehl wrote recently: "At the present time the divergences between Catholicism and Protestantism, which in the 16th century concerned the whole of the Christian message, no longer concern more than a single chapter of doctrine — ecclesiology."[11] But what a chapter! — quite apart from the fact that one may well wonder whether the original divergences, now supposed to be obsolete, are not still reflected in it. The work has already started, at all levels from top to bottom. May God, who has given us to begin the work, grant us to carry it on "wherever he wills, by whatever means he wills."

---

11. Mehl, in *Foi et Vie* (Jan.-Feb. 1978), p. 55.

A letter from Oceania

*John Garrett**

Suva, Fiji

Dear Wim:

This is to recall, on the occasion of your eightieth birthday, that several early explorers of the region between Australia and Easter Island were your countrymen. The greatest was Abel Tasman. Europeans called his contacts with the islands of Oceania "discoveries"; in reality they were *contacts*. Oceania had been found and populated long before by proud migrants with a genius of their own. It seems unlikely that at this period of your life you will come out here along Tasman's track. This letter from someone who once travelled with you in the little ship of the World Council will help you to chart some of the changes that have come about here in recent years — and our hopes for years to come.

Oceania is the least familiar part of the Third World. Ignorance of Polynesia, Melanesia, and Micronesia is widespread. It is difficult to find good maps of island groups which have recently become independent nations, such as Western Samoa, Fiji, and Papua New Guinea. Tourist mythology depicts smiling islanders under palms by azure lagoons; but Nouméa, Suva, Papeete, and Honolulu are multi-cultural cities containing varieties of uprooted people, many of whom work for governments or transnational corporations. They mostly want a better slice of the big cake of economic development. It is easy to advocate zero growth in a penthouse in Brussels; people who live in crowded housing here on less than a hundred dollars a week are not so interested in those theories. William Temple and others used to present Christianity as a faith speaking of a material incarnation and of a just deal in this world for the poor. This makes sense in the Pacific now.

The islands of the South Pacific, taken together, are a Christian area, more so than Latin America, probably more than Finland or Greece. The new na-

---

* Dr. JOHN GARRETT teaches church history at Pacific Theological College, Suva.

tions here have secular democratic constitutions modelled on India; but visitors are surprised to find big meetings opening with long prayers and grow hungry during the lengthy graces offered before island feasts. Here the spiritual remains real; religion was and is important in life. An awareness of a world of spirit and spirits links pre-Christian with Christian religion.

The linkage was certainly ensured in part by the large numbers of islander missionaries who were born here. Eleven hundred names are written in a book on the communion table in the chapel of the Pacific Theological College in Fiji. The white missionaries who led these local planters of pandanus-and-palm-root to Christian faith were carefully commemorated by their boards and societies. We know about their travels and successes (though less about their failures). They, however, did not keep such careful account of the names and deeds of the many Pacific islanders who did most of the day-to-day work ensuring church growth: Tahitians in the Cook Islands and Samoa; Cook Islanders and Tongans in Samoa and across Melanesia; Samoans in the Ellice Islands (now Tuvalu) and the Gilberts (now Kiribati); Tongans in Fiji and as far westward as Papua New Guinea; Fijians in the Solomon Islands and New Britain. Most evangelization in Oceania has been by islanders for islanders. Oral history and careful study of documents will help us to increase and correct the list in the PTC chapel. Such work can now best be done by people who were born here.

For those of us who came here from outside the islands, the rewriting of this history is a service to the truth. Pacific island Christians are less surprised by the evidence than others. They learned in youth from their forebears that the gospel came through other island-dwellers to their families across leagues of sea. In many villages there are oral traditions of islander missionaries who lived in the style of the host country, intermarried, bore children, and settled down. In the Cook Islands, Christianity was first called the Tahitian worship. In Fiji the Wesleyan Church was first called the Tongan worship; many of its founder missionaries were Tongans. Christian missionary migrations shaped regional awareness. The Pacific Conference of Churches counts on this deep underlying sense of identity. Hawaiians were missionaries to Kiribati, the Marshalls,and the Carolines. Many different churches of Polynesia, including minuscule Niué's church, took part in winning the peoples of Papua New Guinea, now the region's largest independent nation. The ecumenical movement was incipient in the Pacific through the form of the mission.

The work of the World Council of Churches has built on this pre-history of unity since the first conference of Pacific island churches and missions at Malua Theological College in Western Samoa in 1961. By 1966 the Pacific

Conference of Churches (PCC), which came out of that meeting, held its first assembly on Lifu, in the Loyalty Islands of New Caledonia. In the same year the Pacific Theological College, a regional training institution for the ministry at advanced level, commenced classes at Suva, Fiji. The college developed faster than the PCC. Mission boards and societies helped to plan and fund it. The Theological Education Fund — now the WCC's Programme on Theological Education — made a large first grant and remained as supporter and guardian angel.

The priority the Pacific churches gave to the PTC was providential. Now, fourteen years later, graduates of the college have become office-bearers and staff members of the PCC. Other graduates are principals and faculty members of local theological schools, such as Samoa's Malua College, Tonga's Siata'outai, the Bethany Pastoral School on Lifu, the Bishop Patteson Centre in Solomon Islands, and the theological college of the Kiribati Protestant Church. Many graduates of the PTC have studied abroad in America and Europe. Assemblies of the Pacific Conference of Churches sometimes look embarrassingly like rallies of former PTC students. The best result of the PTC's work has been the appearance of many able ministries at rural, urban, and administrative levels. Pilot experiments in evangelism, renewal of worship, lay training, and social and political responsibility are multiplying. A woman faculty member supervises a programme for women, fully integrated into regular teaching and into extension courses in other parts of the region.

Lorine Tevi of Fiji is now the General Secretary of the Pacific Conference of Churches — the first woman to be the chief executive of a regional Christian body. Her training and experience in Fiji and the United States fitted her to be a roving interpreter within and beyond the Pacific. She is convincing people in Geneva that the Christian churches of the Pacific islands can bring to the ecumenical movement special qualities different from those found in Asia, Africa, Latin America, and the Caribbean.

Two people who have both studied the map and lived in the Pacific for longer periods have helped to create this awareness — Rex Davis of Australia and Hans-Ruedi Weber of Switzerland. Rex Davis, when he was at the Pacific desk of the WCC, came to know many Melanesian and Polynesian leaders in church and politics. Several times he put up with uncomfortable journeys, unfamiliar food, long unstructured talks late at night, and occasional dysentery. He gained good understanding of the mosaic of populations in this part of the world — and of the slow processes of listening and consensus so different from clock-dominated Rules of Order. Hans-Ruedi Weber has brought with him biblical wisdom, skill as a teacher, and the capacity to listen (the last of these three is in short supply among some ecumenical and denominational ambassadors, who come on short visits, equipped with money but not with grasp, and are sometimes manipulated for local advantage by favourites).

The influence of the Pacific Conference of Churches in many churches and islands has grown with the years. When President Pinochet of Chile started out, early in 1980, to visit President Marcos of the Philippines, he planned to spend two days enroute in Fiji as a guest of the government. The executive committee of the PCC criticized the visit to Fiji, and its members declared that the PCC would not accept invitations to public events in Pinochet's honour, since he was known to be head of a regime that violates human rights. The Fiji Council of Churches followed with a full-page declaration to the same effect signed by heads of churches. The Prime Minister of Fiji, Ratu Sir Kamisese Mara, was at first offended by the churches' "unforgiving" affront to normal protocol. When Pinochet landed at Fiji's international airport he was greeted by a large protest demonstration attended by trade unionists and some clergy. By then he had learned that Marcos had withdrawn the invitation to the Philippines for reasons later revealed to be connected with "security." Pinochet then decided not to attend the public functions arranged by Fiji, cut his visit short, and went home. By that time the Fijian Prime Minister had received from the PCC full documentation describing violations of human rights in Chile. He announced that he had meant to put this evidence before Pinochet personally, with strong words of criticism. He promised to pass on the facts in his hands to the Chilean government through normal diplomatic channels.

Such united action by the churches, including the Roman Catholic Church, would not have been possible in the Pacific twenty years ago. Some observers say the churches have been politicized; but interventions of this kind are made irrespective of political alignments. Loyalty to the gospel also transcends personal piety and the longing for the salvation of individual souls. Christians in the Pacific feel they are becoming an extended family.

Many members of that family are poor. They have little land, little opportunity to break out and live, limited effective power for good. They are pleased when their leaders contend together for the rights of the poor everywhere, in the name of Christ who was himself poor. Their strong waves of approval can be sensed in casual conversations. In the villages people hear what is happening through their transistor radios. They are kept in touch in the middle of the world's largest and loneliest sea. They were glad when the churches spoke together often about French atomic testing in Tahiti. The work of protest was not directed only against France, but against all such tests. Long before France exploded anything in the Pacific the British and American governments had set off worse devices with bigger fall-out at Christmas Island, Eniwetok, and Bikini. The voice of the World Council of Churches, united with the pronouncements of the Holy See, speaks to islanders about what they have seen — ruined crops and lagoons, deformities, deported populations, dead animals and fish. The word Pacific seems like a bad joke. The big powers treat this ocean as a "defence perimeter." On that perimeter people have suffered, and could suffer again, as a convenient shield held in front of the rich. The PCC has consistently said this is abuse of the weak by the strong.

The 1970s have been a decade of Pacific nationalisms. The transfers of power to the new mini-states have been mainly peaceful. Much has been done by committed Christian leaders, including pastors and priests. This is the story in Western Samoa, Niué, Fiji, Kiribati, Solomon Islands, and Papua New Guinea. Some of Papua's hardest-hitting and most controversial cabinet ministers trained under Patrick Murphy, a missionary of the divine word with prophetic foresight, who became the coordinator of the PCC's Church and Society Programme and who died tragically in a road accident at Port Moresby two years ago. Ministers and priests, some of them graduates of the Pacific Theological College, are members of the cabinet and parliament of the emerging nation of Vanuatu — which was, until this year, the surreal Franco-British Condominium of the New Hebrides. Many calm and determined leaders of independence movements in French Polynesia and New Caledonia have been helped in their thinking by the theological work of SODEPAX (though they might plead ignorance of the meaning of that strange acronym!). Walter Lini, an Anglican priest, will be Vanuatu's first prime minister. Gérard Lemayng, a Roman Catholic priest, has been the leader of the French-leaning opposition. The two men were united in their desire to see justice for their people and to abide by the result of democratic elections. Their underlying convictions have helped them to disengage their country from a curious kind of tutelage.

What has happened to the relationships of Roman Catholics and other Christians in the Pacific since Vatican II? Changes in the liturgy, the shape of mission, the status of bishops, lay activity, and ecumenical work have been much the same as elsewhere. The Roman Catholic Church is a full member of the PCC. More specific to Oceania has been the sensation of relief on small islands. People who are of different churches but interrelated through kinship systems have been able to worship together and help each other at last, with the approval of their church leaders. Divided Christians who live on large land masses can alleviate feelings of being oppressed by travelling easily to join sometimes with others of their own group elsewhere. This is harder to do when the nearest Christians of the same denomination are thousands of sea-miles away and the cost of a journey is high. Because this is so the new spirit has come as a Godsend to many islands.

The Roman Catholic bishops of Oceania further improved the situation when they chose a site within walking distance of the Pacific Theological College for their Pacific Regional Seminary. Future Protestant ministers, who are in many cases married persons with families, can share some classes and join in worship. People trained in both institutions fan out when they graduate to serve in their own countries as friends. The encounter brings some challenges for both student bodies and teachers. The question of the possibility of a married diaconate and priesthood comes up in the minds of Roman Catholics. On the Protestant side the new "noble simplicity" of Roman Catholic liturgies, and Catholic biblical renewal associated with the new ways of observing the church year, pass silent judgment on the sloppy disorder in some decadent churches supposed to be loyal to the Reformation.

What of youth? Most people in most islands are now under thirty. Many of them attend church regularly. Belief in God, the faith of their families, remains important in the lives of encouraging numbers of professional people and civil servants. Among others secularism makes progress — though not as yet to any great extent in the Marxist form present elsewhere in the Third World. Dialectical materialism thrives in swollen industrial cities and among desperate peasants. There is so far no visible Mao of the Pacific who has made sense of Marxism as a practical way of changing a world of separated islands. Here Engels and Lenin would have to rethink their positions.

Extremes of wealth, though we have them, are not so distressingly obvious. Simply built houses, verdant fruit-trees, prolific crops, seas full of fish, have helped to make possible, in times of necessity, an economic condition called by some observers subsistence affluence. The seeming happiness of such a life, however, can hide a deeper resentment and loneliness among those who never travel the world's rich highways. Some pioneers have helped chosen villages develop with dignity in their own way and pose their own questions to the governments and developers who try to structure their lives for them. Ruth Lechte of the World YWCA, who is based in Fiji, has given a lead in many parts of Oceania, which she now knows well. Sitiveni Ratuvili of the Pacific Conference of Churches, a PTC graduate, has done the same service to villages in various island countries, along with his wife Watalaite. Through having their worship make sense in their daily life and economic forward planning, the ecumenical movement is assisting people to find their own authentic pathways to hope.

You may be asking by now whether there are signs of the emergence of a good theology, spelled out within the Pacific for the world? The answer is yes, signs... To be a good theology, what eventually comes to the surface must be something more than the familiar, old, borrowed theology in fancy local dress. Reading and writing came later to the Pacific than to other parts of the Third World. The signs of a coming Pacific theology are seen in speech and in gesture. Hendrik Kraemer, if he could have come out here along Tasman's sea-track, would have seen clearly what is coming to birth. His pupil Hans-Ruedi Weber will tell you that it is so. Yams and taro, mango, coconut cream — these local realities have more in common with the fertile life of Canaan than any objects regularly handled at Tübingen, Harvard, or Birmingham. The sea is a wilderness; the shore is promised land. Preachers know what it is like to be fishermen, to toil all night catching nothing, then turn to the Lord for the resolution of human frustrations. The festival of first-fruits and celebration of the ancestors within the communion of saints have reality about them independent of the liturgy. The strife with evil spirits still has immediacy in the Pacific; the victorious Christ, when he prevails, becomes equally immediate in the life of believers.

In Melanesia whole villages still walk through the waters of local rivers to claim the promises in baptism. New ways in holy communion are suggested by the communal feast and the joy of the village round the kava bowl. The library shelves at the Pacific Theological College hold theses and projects written by island students who are trying to embody these signs of a new theology in accordance with alien scholastic rules. In another two decades the straitjacket will be thrown off. Pacific islanders will write for church and world as D.T. Niles used to preach. The principal at the Pacific Theological College, Sione 'Amanaki Havea of Tonga, is a Polynesian chief of his students, guiding those who confidently look to the time when Oceania will bring treasure from the sea for the church of God.

Economic neo-colonialism, hidden racism, and the activities of some denominational adventurers raise problems for the churches in the Pacific. Neo-colonialism tends to turn private enterprise into monopoly and to subjugate small national economies. Its worst feature is its assumption that the only right destiny for all the finely wrought cultural achievements of island cultures is to be gathered up into a global metropolis of concrete and computers, presided over by men in pin-striped suits who live on expense accounts. The maligned original colonialists often stayed long enough to love and learn.

Racism in this part of the world has often been white, but today it is more complicated. A tendency to measure all the world by the cultural convictions of one's own island is strong. The virus of unexamined prejudice is present below the surface in the churches when Polynesians, Melanesians, and Micronesians meet, or when Indo-Fijians and Fijians gather together in Fiji. New Caledonia, with its infusions of Indochinese migrants, offers another test case. The method of combating latent racism will need to be more like preventive medicine than "combat."

As for denominationalism, small islands where one tradition dominates are happy hunting-grounds for builders of confessional empires. The main world confessional bodies recognize the danger; they have turned bravely away from such business. Some have done marvels in the Pacific, notably Anglicans and Lutherans, in ecumenical sharing and concern. But individual promoters, some from within mainline churches, others from smaller "faith" groups, still offend most Pacific Christians by their attempts to make the walls between us reach to heaven. They deny to members of the family, made one in the Pacific by Christ's work, the fuller knowledge they crave of a gathered company without opaque partitions.

The future, we hope, will bring more of the spirit of the islands, welcoming love towards storm-tossed travellers, into the Universal Church. Probably you will not yourself voyage here physically in Abel Tasman's wake; but your name is spoken here gratefully and always will be. The little ship you once steered sails on in the Pacific.

As ever,

John

A mirror for the ecumenical movement?
Ecumenism in Latin America

José Miguez-Bonino *

There is no history of the ecumenical movement in Latin America.[1] As a matter of fact, there is scarcely any history of Christianity in the subcontinent.[2] I have neither the time nor the competence to try to fill this gap. I can only try, in this article, to meditate on a story partly gathered from documents and brief articles but mostly personally lived (and suffered!) in Latin America and in the "ecumenical movement" during the last thirty years.

Latin America in the "oikoumene"

Since its "discovery" in the fifteenth century, Latin America has existed in a condition of dependence in relation to the European (later European-North American) world. The "emancipation" of the Latin American countries at the beginning of the 19th century shifted dependence from the decadent Iberian empire to the rising British one, from direct political to indirect economic control. Latin America was incorporated into the expanding

* Prof. JOSÉ MIGUEZ-BONINO is professor at the Institute of Higher Theological Studies in Buenos Aires, and a President of the WCC.

1. CELEP (Centro Evangélico Latinoamericano de Estudios Pastorales, Apartado 1307, San José, Costa Rica, CA) has published two *cahiers* (Año 1, No. 2, 1978, and Año 2, No. 1, 1979) with several studies in the history and interpretation of Latin American ecumenism. *Cristianismo y Sociedad* (Buenos Aires) published an issue on "Ecumenism in Latin America" (No. 60, 1979). See also "Reflexiones críticas sobre Puebla y Oaxtepec" (3a./4a. entrega 1979). Personally, aside from the articles in these issues, I have tried partial presentations in *Integración Human y Unidad Cristiana* (San Juan, Puerto Rico: Ed. "La Reforma," 1975); "Visión del cambio social y sus tareas desde las iglesias no-católicas," in *Fe Cristiana y Cambio social en América Latina* (Salamanca: Sígueme, 1974); "A Latin American Attempt to Locate the Question of Unity," in *The Ecumenical Review*, XXVI, No. 2 (April 1974), 210-21. In *Geschichte des Christentums in Lateinamerika* (see following note), H.J. Prien has gathered the most relevant information (esp. pp. 885-934).

2. I refer, naturally, to systematic and critical historical studies. The two most important works are E. Dussel, *Historia de la Iglesia en América Latina* (Barcelona: Editorial Nova, 1973) and H.J. Prien, *Die Geschichte des Christentums in Lateinamerika* (Göttingen: Vandenhoeck und Ruprecht, 1978).

capitalist-industrial economy: it was part — a dependent and subsidiary part — of the "Anglo-Saxon oikoumene." The era after the two world wars nevertheless introduced, within the same relation of dependence, some new elements which are worth taking into account.

Three modifications were evident very early in that period. In the first place, dependence became increasingly visible. It was felt, not only by a few discerning minds, but by ever-growing sectors of the population. Second, all sectors were integrated into the world economic system (even rural and previously isolated areas), and the domination extended more and more clearly into the political and cultural areas. Third, the "centre" concentrated more and more in the USA with the decline of Europe and particularly the demise of the British Empire. It is the time of the "American oikoumene."

Important economic and social consequences followed. At the economic level, some countries began to develop some (light) industries to substitute for imports (food processing, textiles, etc.). Later, with the growth of the transnational corporations, many of these industries were taken over or converted according to the international division of labour. All of this also prompted changes in society: growth in urban population; the emergence of a "mass society," made up mostly by the urban sub-proletariat crowded around the big cities; the appearance of an industrial proletariat in some countries and of a middle class, related to commerce, liberal professions, and administration. Politically, the new situation favoured the rise of populisms and the dream of development. In the 1960s, the Cuban revolution inspired a hope of rapid change, but the international interests and local oligarchies made short work of such attempts; and soon a chain of military coups, legitimized through the doctrine of "national security," established a tight control on several nations.

This background is indispensable for understanding the history of Christianity in Latin America in this period. Protestantism — to which I shall limit my comments — was born and grew in our subcontinent in a relation (mostly one of conflict) to Roman Catholicism. The Catholic Church was engaged, at the opening years of our period, in what has been called "the New Christendom" strategy, an effort to recover its integrating and leading role in the new modernizing Latin American society through the organized effort of lay elites imbued with Catholic social doctrine and the neo-Thomist philosophy of Jacques Maritain. But already in the 1950s new trends began to appear: the "French model" of Catholic action, more "secularized," began to be substituted for the more clerical Italian one. The biblical and liturgical renewal reached some seminaries. The "new humanism" of Lebret opened the question of a theology of development.

Then John XXIII and Vatican II exploded throughout the Catholic world. The Latin American Conference of Bishops, meeting in Medellin in 1968, translated the Council into a prophetic engagement for a radical transformation of Latin American society. And Protestantism suddenly found itself confronted with a new Catholicism — a Catholicism with an open Bible, evangelical preaching, lay participation, an ecumenical attitude, and a deep concern for a transformation of society. At the close of the third decade, nevertheless, a wind of conservatism began to sweep through some sectors of Catholicism. The "new Christendom" project was revived. A cautious attitude towards ecumenical relations characterized the last meeting of the episcopate (Puebla, 1979) and the attempt to control "prophetic excesses" characterized some national hierarchies. Protestantism, long dominated by an "anti-Catholic complex," then challenged by Catholic renewal, is now somewhat bewildered and caught up in some of the tensions which exist in the Catholic Church.

Naturally, Protestantism itself has not been static during these three decades. Perhaps the most important development is the phenomenal growth, in this new "mass society," of the Pentecostal movement. The urban sub-proletariat, an uprooted and rootless population, provided fertile soil for this growth. Pentecostalism, loosely "evangelical" in doctrine, living in closely knit congregations but devoid of stable national or international organizations, now makes up the majority of Protestantism. Towards the end of this period it began to discover its own unity and to try forms of continental articulation. Almost totally absent from the First Latin American Protestant Conference in 1949, timidly present in the Second (1961), it was massively present and active at the Fourth Conference (1978) — the second confessional group in numbers.

It has become customary to use the expression "conservative Protestantism" for the vast sector of the Protestantism which originates in the American churches and groups shaped by the revivalist movements and the theological fundamentalism of the nineteenth century. This designation is as sociologically and theologically inadequate as the terms "non-historical churches" or "evangelicals," which are sometimes used. Perhaps the nomenclature suggested by Lalive d'Epinay,[3] who calls these churches "established conversionist sects," although almost exclusively sociological, is the least equivocal. In Latin America it designates primarily the churches generated by the missionary work of North American missionary societies or

---

3. Ch. Lalive d'Epinay, *Les protestantismes latino-americains: un modèle typologique* (Mexico: CIDOC, 1968).

groups, coming particularly from the West and South of the USA, who began their work after World War I, but whose missions escalated, both in the number of groups and of missionaries, after World War II and even more after the closing of the missions in China and other Asian countries.[4] The China experience, the "cold war," and later the Korean war, definitely made an ideological impact on these groups, an impact strengthened by the almost total control of these churches by missionaries from the USA.

Although some of these churches participate in the national councils or federations of Protestant churches and cooperate in evangelistic efforts, their ecumenical ties are very weak. It is more important to note, nevertheless, that a new national leadership began to develop in the 1950s.[5] It is from these Latin American cadres that a theological renewal has begun to develop in the 1960s, as witnessed by the creation of the "Latin American Theological Fraternity," the II CLADE (Conference on Evangelism), and the significant prophetic rôle that some Latin American "evangelical" theologians played at the Lausanne Congress on World Evangelism (1974).

It is equally difficult to find an appropriate nomenclature for the "historical," "ecumenical," or "liberal" churches. Lalive distinguishes three groups, which we will here consider together: the "ecclesia of a transplanted Protestant immigration," "the denomination established among Protestant immigrants," and the "missionary denomination" (or "traditional Protestantism"). Whether originating in immigratory currents or in the missionary work of foreign (Anglo-Saxon) denominations, these churches were planted in Latin America before 1914, and their growth and

---

4. Some figures, gathered by P. Damboriena, S.J., are in themselves quite telling. Between 1949 and 1961 the number of missionaries increased from 3821 to 6451. In 1958 28.49% of all USA missionaries were located in Latin America (second only to Africa, with 35.07%, while Asia had only 10.40%). Finally, if we take the two Latin American countries with the largest number of missionaries in proportion to population, Brazil and Peru, we find that in 1960, of a total of 1428 missionary agents, 1138 belonged to the church type that we are considering for Brazil; the corresponding numbers for Peru were 714 out of 733.

5. While the number of foreign missionaries nearly doubled between 1949 and 1961, the number of national ministers (in the different categories) multiplied by 5. While the percentage of nationals to the total number of church workers in 1949 was 65%, it escalated to 84% in 1961. In Brazil alone, 13,000 new ministers were consecrated or ordained during this period. Although the directive jobs in the training of the ministry, literature, religious education, administration, and supervision were still at the time in the hands of foreigners, the growth of national leadership made itself increasingly felt and assumed responsibility during the last few years. It is true that they sometimes simply prolonged the missionary policies, but not a few began to find their Latin American identity.

institutional consolidation took place before the beginning of the period under consideration. They had developed their schools, seminaries, and publishing houses. At the end of the 1950s a slow convergence began to develop between the two streams: the immigrant communities generated their own national ministries while the missionary churches, arriving at the middle class, reached a similar sociological stratum. A certain cultural affinity, which renders both receptive to the same theological and ideological tendencies, created a space in which ecumenical relations could develop.

Ecumenism in Latin America

Several reasons help to explain the divided, dividing, and divisionist character of Latin American Protestantism: the characteristics of some of the (dissident) churches which began missionary work in these lands; the religious conditions obtaining in Latin America, which forced a polemical stance; the diverse origins of the churches; the conflict between mother- and daughter-churches, aside from "independent Latin American variables," such as the different social conditions characteristic of the different churches; the tension between regions within the subcontinent; and ideological polarization. We have suffered from the reflection of conflicts in the lands of origin of our churches, particularly the fundamentalism/modernism issue and, in the time we are considering, the ecumenical/anti-ecumenical battle. These conflicts, though imported, have been superimposed on the life of Latin American Protestantism.

This does not mean that there has not been in Latin American Protestantism an ecumenical concern or significant efforts to overcome conflicts and divisions. John A. Mackay has rightly pointed out that an ecumenical stream dates back to the very origins of Latin American Protestantism, including significant leaders like Erasmo Braga and Arcadio Morales, and regrets that external pressures and influences caused these early ecumenical efforts to miscarry. But we do not deal only with isolated episodes or persons: Latin American Protestantism has sought to overcome its separateness — if not always its divisions — in a number of ways.

In a stage previous to the three decades under consideration, and dating back to the Panama Missionary Conference (1916), a number of councils or federations of churches were created under the influence of North American mission boards and churches. Several of them, nevertheless, were born in the 1950s (Costa Rica, 1950; Bolivia, 1955; Colombia, 1950; Ecuador, 1949; Guatemala, 1953); and others were restructured or reorganized during that time (Brazil, Mexico, Panama, Puerto Rico, Colombia, Argentina, and Uruguay). The purposes explicit in their constitutions give a clear clue to the nature of the unity that was sought: cooperation, common representation before official governmental authorities, the defense of religious liberty and cooperation in evangelism, religious education, and service. Most of them explicitly exclude "faith and order" issues and refer to "a spiritual as opposed to organic unity."

As a matter of fact, the defense of religious liberty has been one of the dominant concerns and business of the councils. It is a sort of pragmatic ecumenism: a common front, a place of fraternal encounter, an instrument for inter-church cooperation on immediate programmes without mutual questioning or intensive search for a common faith and mission. Several of these councils were related to the International Missionary Council and to the USA Committee on Cooperation in Latin America (CCLA); and a few of leaders (mostly missionaries) were present in the IMC conferences in Jerusalem and Tambaran. But such participation did not seem to have any deep impact in the life of the councils or the churches.

A new stage in the ecumenical "development" — a dependent development, as in other areas — began in the 1950s. The traditional missionary churches, originating from the USA, began to receive the impact of European thought, both through the ecumenical movement and neo-orthodox theology. The latter timidly entered some of the more "progressive" seminaries and drew the attention of young seminarians and students, disenchanted with the narrowness of their pietistic tradition and dissatisfied with the kerygmatic shallowness of liberalism. The Student Christian Movement, under the leadership of Valdo Galland — a Swiss-Uruguayan Reformed minister who had studied in French Switzerland and took charge of the Latin American secretariat of the World Student Christian Federation — began in the late 1950s a series of conferences, study encounters, and publications which projected the thought of the European ecumenical movement. Some of the younger missionaries (Richard Shaull is the outstanding example) initiated a vigorous renewal, which combined the new theological insight with a concern for society. Thus new Latin American leadership emerged in the Protestant churches (particularly in the southern cone of Latin America, but also in Mexico, Puerto Rico, and Cuba), with a new theological vision and a burning ecumenical concern. This would shape ecumenism in the 1960s.

We can begin to measure the nature of this impact by comparing the first two Latin American Evangelical Conferences of Buenos Aires (1949) and Lima (1961). The shift is noticeable from the very themes of the conferences. The 1949 meeting centred on "Protestant" ("Evangelical" is the word used) Christianity in Latin America: it was an affirmation of the reality of Protestantism in these lands. It rejoiced in its growth, asserted its full right to be an integral part of the life of the Latin American people, declared with utmost emphasis (not without some aggressiveness) its conviction over against any possible curtailments of its freedom, and presented itself as a valid alternative to a formal and static Roman Catholicism. The preparatory documents, written by Baez Camargo, Rembao, Mergal, and translations of Hoffet and Merle Davies, reflect these positions. In Lima, on the other hand, the theme was "Christ, the Hope for Latin America": a call to evangelization and to the insertion of Protestantism into the human problematics of Latin America. We do not find here a Protestant apologetics but a confession of faith and mission. The preparatory materials also moved in this direction: a theological exploration of the message, a study of the situation of man and society.

The theological sections of both conferences confirm this impression. We can characterize the 1949 theology as "evangelical liberalism" and the 1961 one as "evangelical neo-orthodoxy": the differing nouns represent the theological structure of the sections, the consistent adjective emphasizes the Christocentric and missionary ethos which controls theological thinking. The relation between theology and situation is much more visible in 1961. The 1949 Message reproduced almost verbatim, in its earlier paragraphs, the declaration of an Asian ecumenical conference; the 1961 Message, by contrast, tried to articulate an understanding of the Latin American situation and of the mission of the church in terms of a Christology built around the concept of the Incarnation and the Lordship of Christ, focusing within this framework the classical themes of the evangelical witness: the redemption from sin and the experience of the living Christ.

The problematics of unity was also presented in an increasingly organic way. The 1949 Conference seemed to concentrate on proving that there was no hidden agenda of organic unity behind the Conference (there was an insistence on "cooperation" and "spiritual unity" and an explicit declaration that "we have not sought, nor do we consider indispensable, an organic, ecclesiastic, or administrative unity"). The 1961 meeting also declared that "structural unity...must not be considered as an absolute goal," but it continued: "we must seek it when, wherever, and in the measure that it is commanded to us in the fulfilment of our task." The 1949 documents spoke of "spiritual unity"; in 1961 the "unity of the body" was the central category, thus trying to overcome the alternatives of spiritualistic and structural unity in terms of the idea of an "organism" (a "body"), visible but dynamic.

Perhaps the most notable difference appears in relation to the Roman Catholic Church. The general tone of 1949 is apologetic: the distinction between "evangelical *faith*" and "Roman Catholic *religion*" (following a book by the Presbyterian missionary W. Stanley Rycroft) pervades the approach. In 1961 this motif is not absent, but the approach is different. Absolute judgments are avoided. It carefully states that "we perceive certain signs of God's action in the movements that take place today within Catholicism." Instead of comparing merits and demerits in both confessions, a theological perspective is established: we are all equally under the judgment and the grace of the one Lord: "We are not led either by an aversion towards Catholicism nor by an attraction to it. In our relation to Roman Catholicism we should follow no other criterion than faithfulness to the gospel." On this basis, it speaks of an openness to dialogue "without false pride or a sense of superiority, without bitterness or resentment" but "without compromising the truth." Protestantism seems to have given up the attempt to justify its existence through the failure or shortcomings of Catholicism: it feels its calling to its proper mission and begins to regard the Roman Catholic Church, not merely as an adversary but also, in the internal diversity which it reflects, as a possible interlocutor.

Finally, we can also compare the shift in the understanding of the Latin American situation. The 1949 vision falls entirely within a "liberal" (in the classic 19th century sense) perspective. The evils from which the continent suffers are those of "underdevelopment" (although this word was not used). This situation, moreover, was attributed almost exclusively to moral causes, in turn dependent on the lack of a mobilizing and progressive religious undergirding. Underdevelopment — now explictly — was the basic category of analysis in 1961. But the term is now related to the social and economic structure: lack of industrial development, investment, diversification of production. There are concrete references to the unjust conditions of the workers and peasants, to the distribution of wealth, to the possession of the land by a few and the need for land-reform. A growing political participation and consciousness is seen as a positive factor: "Our Latin America appears as a continent restless and eager for its evolution and change of structures, hungering for a total transformation."

All these concerns found a vigorous and polemical expression in the 1960s: the ecumenical movements which the Youth Movement (ULAJE) and the Student Movement (the SCMs) had pioneered for almost two decades. There can be no doubt that all these movements (with the possible exception of ULAJE in its earliest expression) were born under the stimulus, and sometimes with the direct support and prompting, of the ecumenical movement. We have already mentioned the work of the WSCF in Latin America. "Church and Society in Latin America" (ISAL, born in Huampani, Peru, in 1961) was clearly related in its origins to the "Church and Society" of the

WCC, and specifically to the programme of study on "the church in rapid social change." MISUR ("Urban Industrial Mission"), originating in a Conference in Buenos Aires, was a counterpart of the similar programme of the WCC. The ecumenical movement, whose Faith and Order concerns had found such a limited reception in the Latin American churches, would exercise a great influence in the area of social thought and commitment through these movements. Unavoidably, it would also be caught in the tensions generated by their radicalization.

Although it is impossible to follow in any detail the history of these movements, a brief comment on one of them will help us to pose one of today's ecumenical problems in Latin America. The first twelve years of ISAL are marked by four continental conferences (1961, 1966, 1967, 1971), in which some fundamental developments took place in search of a greater concreteness. The first is the search for a coherent analysis of Latin American society. While the 1961 meeting oscillated between a developmentalist approach and an understanding in terms of the "sociology of dependence, "the 1966 one clearly and rigorously adopted the latter. Theologically, it articulated its thought around a "theology of history" — deeply indebted to Paul Lehmann and the further developments of Richard Shaull — which tried to interpret "the signs of the times," to find out "what God is doing" in our history. The critique of the churches becomes more specific and incisive. They are accused of having remained "cultural enclaves" within society, not participating in the history of our peoples and therefore unable to understand them.

Between the second and third conferences, these theological and ideological insights received a deeper and more radical formulation in the work of Julio de Santa Ana, particularly in the area of social and cultural analysis, and Rubem Alves. A "theology of liberation" began to be articulated. On the other hand, ISAL, created as an instrument of the churches for reflection on their social responsibility, became a movement committed to social change in Latin America, seeking a strategy and an action of its own. The tension with the organized churches increased: the Third Latin American Evangelical Conference (Buenos Aires, 1969) clearly reflected that tension. A similar process, *mutatis mutandis*, took place in the other movements.

Orlando E. Costas, in a careful analysis of the Third Latin American Protestant Conference, has spoken of "a new vision." He points out that the "socioanalytic language is more precise and committed." It speaks of "a socio-economic inequality between social classes" and calls for "a dynamic and decisive participation of all believers, including ministers, in the processes of transformation of the (existing) political systems." To this new vision belongs also a more self-critical attitude, a recognition of its divisiveness and excessive polemical zeal, of a certain "foreignness" due to its dependence on foreign resources, people, and ideas. In relation to the Roman Catholic Church, the Conference does not merely recognize the renewal that is taking place in it, but confesses the shortcomings of the Protestant churches in the relation to the Catholic Church and rejoices in recognizing that the two communities can participate in God's mission "in this critical time for Latin America."[6]

Costas points out that "a new controversy" also appears in Buenos Aires. In fact, in a covert way, it had been present in the process of preparation for the Conference. A Committee pro-Latin American Protestant Unity had been created in the follow-up of the 1961 Conference. Its leadership, elected by the representatives of the national councils, was largely made up of people related to the ecumenical movement. A campaign accusing the ecumenical movement and the related churches and leadership of leftist leanings had been launched from some fundamentalist quarters, particularly by a few foreign missionaries. The Brazilian Council of Churches, designated by the 1961 Conference as the host for the Fourth Latin American Protestant Conference, hesitated, postponed the dates, and finally cancelled the Conference. The reasons invoked had to do with "the difficulties that the Brazilian organizers had to work with UNELAM" (according to Peter Wagner). It is clear that the critical situation in Brazil, suspicion of the ecumenical leadership, opposition to the "movements" (particularly ISAL) were in the background of the incident. Finally, UNELAM in cooperation with the Argentine Council of Churches organized the Conference. The conflict of theological outlook and commitments was clearly visible throughout the whole process of the Conference. A position paper from ISAL — which participated in the Conference — was severely critical of the churches, challenging their claim exclusively to represent "the community of the Spirit." One of the internal committees of the Conference finally presented a majority and minority report which brought the conflict to the surface. The debate around a theology and a praxis of liberation, the public responsibility of the church in the transformation of society, the political action of Christians, was the decisive line of division. The Conference, unable to reach a decision, received both reports.

---

6. Cf. O. Costas, "Una nueva conciencia protestante: III CELA," in *De Panamá a Oaxtepec*.

This conflict has pervaded the life of the churches and their ecumenical relations for the last twenty years. It was explicit in the Fourth Latin American Protestant Conference (IV CELA, 1978). But a new "ecumenical realism" made itself felt this time. Instead of trying to impose a particular position on the whole Conference, or simply receiving different views, the Conference decided to send back to the churches the issues around which different positions and responses crystallized, and to request the churches that these issues be studied, discussed, and reflected on at the congregational level. Two important convictions underlie this decision. On the one hand, there is a recognition of the artificiality of positions which are defined at a superstructural level (an ecumenical conference, or even a synod or an assembly), but do not represent a living concern and an active engagement of the people whom these declarations are supposed to represent. Secondly, there is the realization that an ecumenical consensus can only be obtained through a "conscientizing" process at the base, where people are able to reflect as Christians on the questions raised in their lives and in the life of their community. Whether these intentions will be realized or not, it is now too early to say. That it is a more fruitful approach than the debate at the top seems to be quite evident.[7]

Latin America in the ecumenical movement?

I have dwelt almost exclusively on the history of the Latin American churches and Latin American ecumenical efforts because it seems to me that this provides a fruitful point of departure for reflecting on the ecumenical situation in world perspective and on WCC problematics and prospects today. In concluding this paper I want to suggest briefly the lines of thought on which I think this reflection can move, the sense in which the Latin American experience of the last thirty years can be "a mirror for the ecumenical movement."

1. If the ecumenical movement in Latin America has largely been an "import" from the Northern world, it is also true that it has developed here within the conditions of Latin American society and churches. Since the late 1960s it has *reacted on* the ecumenical movement at large, posing for it a specific problematics and challenge. The first massive input from Latin America came at the time of the Church and Society Conference in Geneva (1966). In the debate about Christians in the technical and social revolutions of our time a numerous and articulate representation from the Third World (in which the Latin Americans for the first time played an important role) made clear the option for "a more radical or revolutionary position" over against the traditional ecumenical stance of seeking social change "through

7. *Ibid.*, "Documentos de Oaxtepec," pp. 87-132.

quiet efforts at social renewal working in and through established institutions according to their rules," as the Report words it. Greeted by some as a qualitative step in ecumenical thinking, deplored by others as a fall into politicization, it clearly signalled, as a bitter critic of the WCC has said, "a crucial turning point in the WCC's view of the West and its responsibilities to the Third World."[8]

This was indeed a turning point in the relation of Latin America to the ecumenical movement: from an almost purely passive, receptive presence it moved into an active one. But it merely underlined and gave a new expression to what had emerged in the 1960s: the WCC was becoming geographically ecumenical. The presence of Asia, in the first place, had brought back the question of the relation with people of different faiths and the problems of nation building; Africa forced the consideration of racial discrimination and escalated tensions between some of the churches; in Latin America social, political, and economic questions appeared as inseparably related. The traditional Western answers — as articulated in the idea of "responsible society" or the "development" ideology which inspired the first WCC approaches to "rapid social change" — proved unsatisfactory. The question of radical change, ideology, and political involvement could not be postponed.

Not a few people and churches in the West have perceived this change as a threat, a disruptive "politicization" of the WCC. Strangely enough, they did not seem to realize that the Council — and the churches which participated in it — had been politicized all along. In fact, even a cursory reading of the documents of the ecumenical movement of the last fifty years reflects all the tensions and conflicts of the Northern Hemisphere, from the aftermath of World War I to the Cold War and détente, not to mention World War II. Dr Visser 't Hooft's *Memoirs* document in an admirably candid way the deep political involvement of the WCC during its formative years. They make no bones about its partisan position and look on it as an act of Christian obedience — which it undoubtedly was!

The lines of tension and conflict change when the WCC moves beyond the Northern and Western world: the new visions and analyses cannot be accommodated within the existing categories and frameworks; the theological reflection that emerges from them is not a continuous extension of that generated in Europe and the USA. Thus, naturally enough, they create a sense of fear and irritation. In such a situation, some have felt the challenge to forge a new ecumenical vision in the new situation. Others are launching

---

8. Ernest W. Lefever, *Amsterdam to Nairobi: the World Council of Churches and the Third World* (Washington, 1979), p. 25.

the always attractive battle cry of return to the "origins of the movement." Most, perhaps, remain uncertain and somewhat bewildered.

One thing seems clear: in a world divided by race, class, sex discrimination, economic and political domination, no form of the ecumenical movement can avoid struggling with these issues. Whatever we say or do — or neglect to say or do — will play into the dynamics of these conflicts. How can an ecumenical movement live and operate in these circumstances?[9]

2. We have already referred to the two main institutional forms which the ecumenical movement has taken in Latin America. On the one hand are the councils and federations of churches, whose value and strength has been on the decline for the last two decades. By trying to avoid all conflicts — both theological and social — and build on minimal superficial or pragmatic coincidences, they have become irrelevant. It became clear, at the time of the Fourth Latin American Protestant Conference that no lasting ecumenical project could be built on them.

The other model has been the "movements." They chose the opposite line: to articulate a clear and definite theological, ideological, and political option and to organize themselves as committed and active movements within Latin American society.[10] Their contribution to the life and mission of Christianity and to the Latin American struggle for liberation has been very significant and will be seen even more clearly when we have a better historical perspective. For churches which remained introverted and unaware of their responsibilities, these movements have posed the challenge of the gospel and of the real conflicts of our societies. They have shown to the Latin American world — particularly to the forces struggling for change — a new face of the Christian faith, which has shaken some of the anti-religious prejudices and stereotypes in a way that no verbal apologetics could do. They have forged a new ecumenical solidarity within and outside the confessional churches.

Nevertheless, this model too has proved insufficient. The rapid radicalization of small groups — mostly intellectuals — broke the active relation to the

---

9. I have not mentioned the other great "challenge" to the established theology and practice of the ecumenical movement — the massive Orthodox presence, both in its theological and sociological impact.

10. These comments refer only to the movements mentioned earlier, born in the 1940s and 1950s under the ecumenical impact. There are a number of movements related to the "conservative" churches, which have remained more closely related to their constituency, but which in the last decade have undergone processes not too distant from the former (cf. the Theological Fraternity, the Intervarsity groups, and CELEP, to mention only a few). The associations of theological institutions belong to a third type, and have fulfilled an increasingly important role, which I am unable to analyze here.

churches (not only to the leadership but more seriously to the membership), while failing to create any significant relation to the "peoples' movements" except to the extent that they cooperated with Roman Catholic groups or movements which had a more direct access to the population. Thus, the movements became in many cases small groups, without a constituency, and with all the temptations of bureaucratization and introversion which such groups face. On the other hand, the brutal repression launched in many Latin American countries against all forces of change has affected some of the groups and reduced the space in which they could operate. Their efforts to unite — since their definitions and programmes coincide almost totally — have not proved successful.

These movements have continued to provide intellectual stimulus, and we should not conclude that their role and effectiveness are over. If they are able to overcome their isolation, to correct some of the bureaucratic tendencies which have blocked their attempts at unity, they may still be a significant force in the ecumenical movement in the continent. But it is also clear that they are not a valid model for the ecumenical movement as a whole nor a solid basis on which the search for unity could grow.

3. This is the situation in which the Fourth Latin American Protestant Conference met in Oaxtepec, Mexico, in September 1978. It had been decided to build on the basis of the churches as the main protagonists; nevertheless, the "movements" were invited and participated actively both in the preparation and in the process of the conference. Although there were some important absences, it was the most representative gathering of Latin American Protestants. All the confessional, historical, and ideological tensions whose historical background we have tried to discuss here were present. Several "ecumenical projects" were competing for supremacy: the old conciliar cooperation, the spiritual unity, the committed ecumenism of the movements, the evangelistic passion which postpones all institutional or social concerns, the quest of organic union.

Was it possible, desirable, legitimate, to create a Latin American Council in these circumstances? Two things seem clear enough: (1) the definite, strong will of all the churches present to create a visible and concrete ecumenical instrument; and (2) the impossibility of coordinating, reconciling or amalgamating these different ecumenical projects. For some, this situation meant that no such permanent instrument should be formed; but the majority clearly felt otherwise. Finally, through a difficult and at times painful process, the Latin American Council of Churches (in process of formation) was created. A period of four years was envisaged in which the process should mature until a constitutive assembly could be held.

The reasoning which underlies this decision seems to me worth pondering for the ecumenical movement as a whole. It turns around two premises. The first is the frank acceptance of the existence of these different, even contradictory "ecumenical projects." No one can claim to represent *the* project of the Council; they cannot be made compatible by some clever dialectics or formula; no one should be requested to tone down convictions for the sake of unity. We have to accept the fact that an ecumenical council (*conseil*) in Latin America is a common house in which a number of nonunifiable ecumenical concerns find shelter. But this is already a task, in fact, it is *the* task of the Council: the possibility of encounter, conversation, confrontation, a tense but potentially fruitful common life which strives to overcome its separateness. A council is, in this sense, a battleground, a place where we accept and welcome the mutual challenge, the risk of "contamination," the mutual "proselytizing" of these different ecumenical projects. We accept living with these contradictions in a house which is not in good order, in which all of us feel at times extremely uncomfortable and never quite at home. But we are committed not to move from under the common roof — the visible sign of the unity which we can deny but cannot destroy. We are committed not to desert the battlefield — the visible sign of the claim of that ecumenical project to which each of us is committed in faith.

The other premise is the conviction that the Council's future depends on its ability to bring the challenge of this difficult situation to the life of the whole people of God in Latin America. The different ecumenical projects are not born in a vacuum: they reflect — positively and negatively — the tensions, struggles, and aspirations of different groups (religious, cultural, ethnic, social) of the Latin American people. Only as Christians in these different situations are able to listen, to enter into, to make their own the questions and struggles of other Christians will the conditions for a common witness be created. Therefore, the authorities of the newly constituted Council were given as their first and almost exclusive task to place all the questions and problems raised at Oaxtepec to the Christian congregations throughout the continent. The churches should not be faced with statements to approve or projects to carry out; they should be confronted with the crucial issues and invited to wrestle with them and share honestly and frankly their responses with each other. Whatever unity is born of this process will not be an idealistically conceived one but — however meagre — a unity based on the actual life and reflection of the people of God.

Is it possible for such a decision to be carried out? Many things militate against it. The churches will not easily lend themselves to be challenged; they will tend to protect their people from dangerous questions. The "movements" will find it difficult to have the humility necessary to let their "enlightened" commitment be questioned by "conservative," "pietistic," or "alienated" churches. The ecumenical agencies overseas will flood the new ecumenical instruments with their projects, offers, and invitations — so difficult to resist when the needs are great and the temptation of power is so attractive. The ecumenical agencies will, in turn, be tempted to make the new Council a local counterpart of themselves. The staff will find it easier and more seductive to organize programmes and projects than to wrestle with the prejudices, the blindness, and the arrogance of many in the churches.

Dare we hope that God's grace can help us to resist the temptations? After all, ecumenical commitment is an act of faith!

No turning back:
Caribbean ecumenism

*Roy G. Neehall**

As regards ecumenical relations and actions, the Caribbean churches, including the Roman Catholic Church and a few evangelical churches, have come a long way in the past fifteen years; but they are ready to admit that they still have a long way to go.

Motivated by an inner conviction that "although our pasts and our traditions have been different, our future can be only one," they have created regional instruments to help shape the future in faithfulness to that conviction. The Caribbean Conference of Churches, with its twin agencies CADEC (Christian Action for Development in the Caribbean) and ARC (Action for Renewal of the Churches), has carved out a place and a role for the regional ecumenical movement in the ongoing struggles of Caribbean peoples for unity, identity, change, justice, and development.

The search for greater Christian unity is consciously charted via participation together in these human struggles, as evidenced in the preamble of the CCC Constitution: "We are deeply concerned to promote the human liberation of our people, and are committed to the achievement of social justice and the dignity of man in our society." In the process of acting towards these goals, the churches' understanding of the dimensions of mission has expanded and their experience of "community" has become a reality.

Impulses have come from deep within the faith and life of the Caribbean churches themselves, although they remained dormant through long periods of colonial domination. Motivation, encouragement, and support for these impulses have come from the world ecumenical movement and the Second Vatican Council. Small steps along the way, as early as 1957, derived no little support from global ecumenical bodies: the World Council of Christian Education, the International Missionary Council, the Theological Education Fund, and the World Council of Churches — especially its Commissions on

---

* Dr. ROY G. NEEHALL has been General Secretary of the Caribbean conference of Churches since its inception in 1973.

World Mission and Evangelism, on Churches' Participation in Development, and on Inter-church Aid, Refugee and World Service, and (in the 1970s) SODEPAX.

Illustrations of how the Caribbean churches have responded to the Caribbean reality in recent years do not tell the whole story. For there is growing evidence that in responding so often together to countless needs, problems, and crises, the several denominations are beginning to experience a new perception of what it means to be Christian at the historical moment in which Caribbean people are cast. The gospel call, with its imperatives for both personal and social life, demands much more than what has been attempted or achieved, but there is real ground for hope today as the movement accelerates into the decade of the 1980s.

The Caribbean reality

The ecumenical response to the gospel has had to try to come to terms with all facets of the Caribbean reality. No longer is the Caribbean a homogeneous replica of metropolitan colonial powers. That image was upset by the movements for independence during the 1960s and 1970s and, more recently, by the many challenges to the neo-colonial political, economic, and social structures presented by radical groups, peoples' movements, and workers' organizations. The old image of the church as the sanctifier of the status quo still lingers in the minds of those who are sceptical about its willingness or ability to be an agent of change. So far the direction taken by the ecumenical movement created by the churches, in its various actions and activities, has stimulated a growing recognition that it is constantly challenging the churches to be agents of change while acting with effectiveness to initiate, support, and defend changes towards greater authenticity and social justice.

The complexity of the Caribbean reality is missed by those whose vision of the region is confined to waving palm trees, beautiful beaches, and happy-go-lucky people, and by those who are solely interested in cheap raw products, land, and labour.

The Caribbean is a microcosm of the Third World, in which the majority of people are descendants of Third World people from Africa and Asia. Besides racial and religious pluralism, increasingly there is ideological pluralism as well. There are many historical and cultural similarities among Caribbean peoples which make them objectively one, but all sorts of influences have prevented them from becoming one in a subjective sense. Included in the region are not only islands that are mainly independent (with a few remaining colonies of Holland, France, and Britain), but also mainland territories of South and Central America. Through these, the Caribbean maintains important links with the Latin American reality.

Another important aspect of life in the Caribbean has been the dominance of American influence. Not only does the USA continue to treat the region as a playground or a back yard, but there is also an increasing US military presence. Movements for change in Jamaica, Grenada, Nicaragua, San Salvador, and Dominica have elicited a sort of American paranoia against the alleged influence of Cuba. Caribbean leaders are protesting the demonstrations of power and stronger military presence that form part of American policy *vis-à-vis* the Caribbean. No longer is it only Cuba, the single Communist state in the Western Hemisphere, but also recent political events, successes of popular movements, and choices in favour of alternatives to the capitalist system elsewhere in the Caribbean, which send shock waves back to Washington.

Within this reality, the image of the church is changing dramatically. In some countries it is recognized as having both the opportunity and the ability to influence political, social, and economic development. In others it is seen, either as institution or through its leaders, to be deeply involved in the struggles of the masses and in popular movements for change. Together, the churches have achieved an unexpected degree of unity in programmes of social action dealing with issues of justice and human rights. Slowly but surely, being in solidarity with the poor, the oppressed, and the underprivileged is influencing the pronouncements and the policies of the Caribbean church and giving substance to the claim of the regional ecumenical movement that it has seriously made "a preferential option for the poor." In the Caribbean these are testing times for such a commitment, but the foundations for a strong Christian movement for social change laid during the past decade seem to be holding well.

Analysis of the response

1. *Fragmentation/Integration:* Regional integration has been projected for some time as an essential ingredient in the process of human development for all the nations of the Caribbean. If achieved, it could lead to a larger measure of self-reliance through sharing and a rationalization of both agricultural and industrial enterprises. The importance of unity within the region has to be understood within the larger context of relations with superpowers and multinational corporations and within the framework of Third World solidarity in the demand for changes in the present economic structures and the eventual establishment of a new international economic order. The effectiveness of such solidarity has been demonstrated by the formation of OPEC.

The building up of unity among the churches of the Caribbean, first through programmes of functional cooperation and, since 1973, through the formation of the Caribbean Conference of Churches, is an attempt to challenge the past fragmentation. Thousands of people at all levels, including the grassroots, are involved in the programmes of the two agencies of the CCC — ARC and CADEC. Their involvement together has meant the crossing of barriers, not only denominational, but also national, geographical, linguistic, and colonial. This is seen as a movement to foster unity at the "people to people" level in order to facilitate regional integration and give a popular base to economic and social cooperation between governments and institutions. The unity promoted by the CCC is not geared to the self-preservation of the churches but to the service of the community.

A new source of fragmentation in the Caribbean today is ideological pluralism. The challenge to the churches is not only to resist the exploitation of this by external forces, but to support changes, whatever their ideological base, which guarantee the rights of all and lead to greater social justice for the poor and the oppressed. We feel that we do not need to get into the game of ideological purity but that theological clarity is much more relevant to the bias of the gospel in favour of the poor.

2. *Poverty/development*: Preoccupation with the symptoms of poverty consumed much of the energy and resources of the Caribbean church in the past; and there is still a healthy response to programmes dealing with charitable works, emergency relief, and welfare. The development agency CADEC has, through its communications and education departments, achieved a significant breakthrough in building up awareness of the causes of poverty. As a result, hundreds of social or economic development projects in agriculture, animal husbandry, fishing, crafts, and vocational training have been started with support from the CADEC Development Fund. Local churches, community groups, rural cooperatives, councils of churches, and even government ministries have been the project carriers. More and more, control over the Fund has been decentralized and grants placed in the hands of national or local development committees, so that many projects do not have to be vetted by anyone other than local people. In fact, the basic principle on which the Fund was established was a challenge to church agencies and other funding bodies in the North Atlantic world, who wanted to share their resources with Caribbean countries but were accustomed to supporting individual projects. This has been an important departure from the method of control exercised by donors. Now all projects are subject to the evaluation of Caribbean people, and the idea of "rules of taking" counter-balances the traditional "rules of giving."

Getting at the roots of poverty inevitably leads to conflicts with existing structures and interest groups. Projects become more than ways of improving standards of living and are recognized as symbols of and effective responses to the challenge that the underprivileged face when they decide to change their situation.

Concrete development programmes have to be backed up by an ongoing process of training, research, documentation, publications, analysis, information-sharing, exchange visits, and expert advice; and all these have been built into the functions of CADEC. Opportunities have to be provided for those involved in action aimed at achieving a better life at the micro-level to use their experience to understand better the forces that work against the poor at the macro-level. Reflection and planning follow, as the struggles to change the structures of domination or injustice continue. Economic inequities may not always be affected by isolated economic development projects, but the lessons learned from them can be applied to the larger structural questions and can lead to the kind of solidarity among those who, up to a few years ago, accepted their plight and their dependency without questioning.

3. *Malnutrition/food production*: Like many parts of the Third World, the Caribbean has a record of malnutrition. In countries like Haiti, the situation is very bad. In some countries the lack of adequate food, especially protein, can be traced directly to the shortage of arable land for food production available to the poorest rural folk. Much of the land is alienated from the people for the production of export crops like sugar, cocoa, bananas, and citrus on large plantations, or because of housing developments for the middle class, or for the development of hotels. When the churches started in the early 1970s to point to this injustice, it became obvious that they would themselves have to set an example. And so CADEC launched an appeal for church lands — in Jamaica first of all, and then in some other territories — to be put at the disposal of peasant farmers for food production. The programme, called Land and Food for People, has brought new hope to thousands of rural folk, and the input into it from outside has been limited to seeds, equipment, and technical expertise. A direct result has been to raise people's awareness of the causes of their health and nutrition problems. This has led to increasing militancy in demanding agrarian reform and a more just land-tenure system. One dynamic project in Dominica, "CASTLEBRUCE," has by its example and support led to the formation of a large number of rural cooperatives across the island. The people involved in this federation of rural cooperatives have become a political force, partly responsible for the resignation last year of the government, which had become oppressive and corrupt. The churches were in the forefront of that struggle and the CCC

provided aid to the people when shortages of foodstuffs made it increasingly difficult for them to maintain their strike.

4. *Oppression/human rights*: When the churches of the Caribbean, through the CCC, take a prophetic stand together on situations of oppression or repression, they can bring to bear a large constituency in several nations, a network of communications resources, financial support from around the world, and technical and legal expertise. Several times in the past seven years, we have been challenged by the churches to support a struggle in a local situation against the violation of human rights or outright oppression. In Grenada, under the brutal dictator Eric Gairy, demonstrations by church leaders, civic organizations, students, and trade unions on the eve of independence failed to secure guarantees for protection against police brutality and violations of basic human rights. A general strike began to put pressure on the government, but the people had to be supported in order to keep it up. The churches appealed for help, and the CCC found ways of providing them money to keep the strike going long enough to secure the guarantees demanded. But all the promises were not honoured, and in the end the government was overthrown. The whole pattern of life has changed, and there is hope that a society based on the principles of justice and equal opportunity will result. As in the cases of Nicaragua and Zimbabwe, there have been no reprisals against former enemies. Help is being secured for projects that are not only providing increasing employment for people but are using the land and human resources for benefits to the poorest rather than for the enrichment of the privileged.

Because of the desperate desire of some governments to remain in power by fair or foul means, all criticism or dissent in such situations is interpreted as subversion. There is suppression of the press to contend with, as well as curtailment of civil liberties, rigged elections, and harassment of opposition groups. Guyana is an example of this. More and more legal aid has had to be found by the churches and other agencies to support those involved in human rights cases. Sugar workers in Guyana, newspaper workers in Trinidad, civil servants in Dominica were all given moral or financial support by the CCC; and their causes were brought to the attention of the whole Caribbean through *Contact* (the monthly paper of the CCC), radio programmes, and public meetings.

The CCC and its member churches joined in an effective protest against Barclay's Bank International for continuing to support the government of South Africa and its para-statal projects through loans. Accounts were withdrawn from Barclay's Bank and transferred to national banks. A campaign was launched against Barclay's, and several churches and individuals followed the example of the CCC. Unhappy about this campaign, the bank distributed counterclaims throughout the Caribbean. That struggle continues with the support of only some churches. Others feel that it is not an effective way to challenge Barclay's alleged financing of apartheid, but that dialogue with Barclay's in the Caribbean could lead to some support for the matter from among the local employees of Barclay's in each territory. Research is continuing into the involvement of Canadian and American banks in the indirect financing of apartheid.

Confrontation with some governments and other institutions in the Caribbean has been inevitable, and for the first time churches that used to be closely tied to the establishment are beginning to experience what it is like to be on the other side. As in so many parts of the Western world, churches, individual Christians, and even bishops and archbishops — anyone who supports the struggle to change the status quo — are being called Communist. What aggravates the situation for the CCC is that we have member churches in Cuba and active participation by Cuban church leaders in all our major committees and programmes.

We have always had racial and religious pluralism in the Caribbean, and it does not bother us — as it seems to bother others — to have ideological pluralism as well. We are searching for an alternative society that would be peculiarly our own, not a carbon copy of some dominant power. Why do so many Christians give the credit for genuine people's movements for change and liberation to Communism? I refuse to concede to the one super-power that the liberation of the poor in the Third World is a Communist ploy, or to the other that Marxism is the only ideology that can generate such liberation.

5. *Colonial mentality/Caribbean identity*: Real development means much more than economic growth. It is possible for a country to have substantial increases in its gross national product year after year and still remain underdeveloped or mal-developed as far as the majority of its people is concerned. More and more, the insistence that many Third World leaders put on values such as human dignity, cultural identity, and self-reliance has been winning support in the West. On the other hand, some Third World countries fail to implement the goals of social and distributive justice, people's participation in the decision-making process, and respect for fundamental human rights.

Caribbean people are plagued by the historical fact of being mainly the products of colonial empire building. Their values have been oriented for years towards those of the metropolitan states. The educational system has prepared them more for life in New York, London, Toronto, Paris, Amsterdam, or Miami, than for the Caribbean. On the island chain one finds people whose orientation is not towards the sea, as in the case of the Pacific islands. They have a metropolitan soul.

For generations, that soul has been dominated by imported Western theology, liturgy, music, hymns, and styles of church life and witness. Even though movements for independence and cultural identity have released many indigenous impulses, and peculiar Caribbean feelings have emerged or come to the surface in everyday cultural life or in folk religions, the life, work, and witness of the people in the traditional churches, as in the many conservative groups, remained but a carbon copy of the mother churches in the North Atlantic.

Now at last, with direction and resources provided by the Renewal Agency of the CCC, changes are taking place which begin with the historical reality, experience, and feelings of Caribbean people and let their creative abilities flow in theological reflection and writings, hymns, music for worship, a new ecumenical curriculum for use in both churches and schools, and extensive programmes of lay training and continuing education for clergy at both national and regional levels. A clearer and deeper understanding is emerging of what it means to be a Christian in the context of Caribbean reality and wider acceptance of what the late Pope Paul VI stressed: that social justice or the liberation of people is a constitutive part of the proclamation of the gospel.

The struggle for economic justice is not just the concern of politicians and international economists; it is a natural ingredient of Christian mission, and the churches of the Caribbean are beginning to accept both the responsibility and the risk of participating in that struggle. The ecumenical movement, in its programmes of reflection and action, gives the Caribbean church a framework for renewal of faith and witness that is setting it free from its colonial status and image.

The future — a critique

The very fact that we can today speak with a measure of confidence about the Caribbean *church* rather than only of the *churches* is evidence that some significant change has taken place in the Caribbean, long regarded as the last bastion of the church of the Middle Ages and the scene of successful denominationalism. We have come a long way, and that is all the more reason why we cannot allow the gains of the recent past to be eroded by the new phenomenon of ideological denominationalism. On the same day of any week of the year, leaders of the same denomination can be heard in different parts of the Caribbean speaking to the same issues that affect the lives of their societies and saying completely conflicting things. Naturally, they agree on doctrinal and faith matters but represent conflicting political and economic ideologies.

In the 1960s there was progress in reducing traditional hostilities and tearing down barriers that separated one church from another. Orthodox denominationalism was dealt a mortal blow. Throughout the 1970s the spirit of ecumenism invaded the churches and issued in various concrete forms of collaboration and various structures of common action at regional and local levels. The Christian Councils, the United Theological College in Jamaica, and the old Caribbean Committee on Joint Christian Action were precursors of this; and the CCC, CADEC, and ARC, are testimonies to the reality that church renewal in the context of Caribbean history, experience, and culture is a requirement for effective witness, and that participation in the development of Caribbean peoples in terms of social justice and liberation is at least intellectually acceptable as a valid part of mission and a constitutive element of the gospel. Emphasis on the social imperatives of that gospel are endorsed in one meeting, document, or pronouncement after another, not only in the rarefied air of ecumenical gatherings but in the down-to-earth sessions of denominational courts. We seem to be on our way.

Now comes the influence of new popular or political movements for change which seem to borrow the pronouncements of the church and then create an ideological framework and political strategy for bringing about the very changes that the church's vision forecasted. The time has come to take sides, and the churches find themselves in the middle of a new history of division. The old divisions are bypassed and we are on the verge of a growing conflict, which arises in every church, between the defenders of the status quo, the critics of the status quo who want change without confrontation, the challengers of the existing systems who want change and see conflict as inevitable, and the radicals who want conflict whether it leads to change or not.

How are we going to deal with this reality? So far we have managed to integrate all these positions in the regional ecumenical movement. We soon discover, however, that in so doing, we run the risk of making the movement wishy-washy, unable to take a firm stand on issues of consequence. What is even more disturbing is that we have not always been able to forge an alliance with other social forces or movements which have the power to implement our dreams of a new Caribbean society.

Perhaps it is the fear that the movement which has become institutionalized may have to face some measure of disintegration so that truth and human liberation may emerge out of the ashes of exploitative systems. We do not want to lose the unity we have, and that can become a dangerous antecedent to losing our credibility.

An alternative society is a must in the Caribbean. That means that all kinds of options, in every area of life, have to be considered. Will the churches confine themselves to encouraging consideration and give no moral support to one option in preference to another? I see the 1980s as the last chance to sit on the fence.

I believe that unity is not only possible on the fence but also in the area of direct social action. However, some things will have to happen within the church itself if the motivation is to become a greater reality. The Caribbean people have to be taken more seriously as a peculiar people. We cannot escape the fact that we act like the colonizers of superior powers in many ways. We think their thoughts and follow their values, but we do not *feel* like them. We should not be ashamed that we often arrive at decisions by a non-linear rather than a logical process of reasoning. Just because people applaud a well-reasoned speech or sermon, it does not follow that they will be guided by its logic.

To put heart back into religion is one of the major challenges facing the church in the Caribbean today. We have intellectualized religion to the point where too many people are made into second-class Christians because they can neither conceptualize nor articulate the faith in patterns of intellectual orthodoxy. If feelings, emotions, and cultural tendencies were taken more seriously there might not now be the big gap between church and home, school, office, business, union, etc. The rapid rise of the charismatic movement in certain mainline churches, particularly the Roman Catholic Church, is a good case in point of the appeal of a spirit-filled, heart-filled approach to religious expression. It has clearly helped to initiate and sustain fundamental renewal of faith and witness among those who in the past were least given to make a public demonstration of their religious emotions and feelings — as, for example, the successful middle and professional classes in Trinidad. Admittedly, this movement is represented by a minority of Caribbean Christians, but their impact on the whole church will no doubt increase in this decade.

At the other end of the scale is another growing movement of discontented and militant poorer people, including many underprivileged youth, who link their religious convictions to a feeling of hurt because the society gives them little hope of development and little chance to share in the benefits that accrue from the resources of the land. Already they have participated in radical movements for change and have helped to generate the power for revolutions in such Caribbean territories as Cuba, Grenada, Dominica, Nicaragua, and Surinam.

Their call to the church for support creates a dilemma for us. Some in the church view the rise of popular labour or armed uprisings in the region as a salutary process. Others say that we are already committed by our pronouncements about a more just society, the well-being of the poorer masses, and the rights of the underprivileged. The problem is compounded by the general commitment among Christians to peaceful and nonviolent ways of achieving desirable change. When the Caribbean church in the 1971 Chaguaramas consultation on development made a clear decision to support the liberation of the poor and the oppressed, there was still the hope that the controllers of political and economic power might see the handwriting on the wall and begin to use more of that power to bring about changes in the structures that oppress the poor. That was only a dream. Now that the frustrated poor have begun to take control of their environment through confrontation, conflict, and force, the question is posed with more urgency: where does the church stand in supporting the new societies being established and — what is even more important — where will the church stand when the call comes, as it will, to lend support to organizations of the poor to effect change at any cost?

An inevitable corollary to all this, which we are learning from experience, is that the church must also make up its mind about where it stands when the backlash comes. Such resistance to change takes a variety of forms, as we are witnessing in the Caribbean: subtle destabilization of the movements of the poor and the new societies that emerge after radical change is effected, economic sanctions, orchestrated denigration in the press within the region and abroad, withholding of development aid or the threat of no new aid unless certain conditions are met, and, what is even more alarming, the determination of the US government to bring the region into line, as has been made clear in the decisions of Washington. One only has to read President Carter's speech of October 1, 1979, concerning the presence of Soviet troops in Cuba, to conclude that direct and aggressive forms of geopolitical manoeuvring will be the order of the day in the 1980s, made necessary because of the rapidly changing dynamics in the region, which, in turn, represent potential threats to the "climate of stability" so important to financial investments — that is, to the Western capitalist system. In a recent address in Barbados George Lamming denounced the "system of economic and cultural imperialism" which continues to exist in the region "in profound conflict with the struggle of labour for an alternative society."

It is in the gospel of Jesus Christ that I find the motivation for the commitment that the Caribbean church has made to live and act in solidarity with the poor and oppressed and to participate in their efforts to liberate themselves and to achieve a measure of human dignity and development.

"Poverty," writes Neville Linton, "cannot be successfully attacked without methods that, on the political side, cannot always be peaceful or fully democratic or without political confrontation. On the economic side, poverty cannot be attacked without some inefficiency and wastage, without projects which are self-financing, are non-economic or involve financial losses, and without many failures and false starts, just as the national wealth around the developed world was created with exactly these same political and economic costs.''

The Caribbean church and the instruments of ecumenical cooperation which it has created — CCC, CADEC, and ARC — have opted to be and to act during this decade in solidarity with the poor of the region. We need to anticipate the dilemmas this option brings and to estimate the cost as we plan our strategy. Experience over the past two decades provides many of the answers, and we must make up our accounts in terms of plus and minus factors. In his first sermon Jesus said, ''Repent, for the kingdom of heaven is at hand'' (Matt. 4:17). That is the message of the church to the world. How much evidence is there in the way Christians live to support our claim that the kingdom of heaven is at hand?

Everyone sees that we have serious problems in the Caribbean church not just because of past history but because of our image. Fundamental change is accepted as a necessity but there the agreement often ends. Some stress *kerygma*, preaching the gospel or renewal through evangelism; some stress *charisma*, filling by the Holy Spirit and the experience of the Spirit's gifts, renewal by charismatic experience. Some stress *diakonia*, service to the poor or service and political action on behalf of justice; some stress *propheteia*, the challenge of the king, or acts of resistance to the power and violence of the authorities.

In a sense all of these emphases can claim foundation in Scripture and Christian tradition. But there is a fifth that makes real sense in the region in which the Caribbean church lives. It is *koinonia*, community, the call simply to be the church, to love one another, and to offer our lives for the sake of the world. It is the ongoing life of a community of faith which issues a basic challenge, in a region where the sociologists say we have never known community, to be recognized as a visible and concrete alternative. Unless that can become a reality in the 1980s we may succeed in doing a lot for the poor but not in establishing solidarity with them or capitalizing on the tremendous potential of the pluralistic nature of the region. The basic communities of faith may well become the integrating force that generates both renewal and social change, rather than the image that the local congregations often have of being ghettos of religious isolation. Then perhaps the poor will have the opportunity to minister to the rich and the powerful and to cause the kind of active and meaningful repentance which must precede the establishment of God's kingdom on earth.

Finally, the 1980s will raise serious questions about the credibility of the Caribbean church in the face of the needs and problems of the poorest of our people. If we are not prepared to change our life-style, our links with centres of power, our neutrality on political issues, and our fear of conflict, it would be better to choose another option rather than solidarity with the poor. If, however, we are faithful to the gospel, we cannot but go with that option and face the consequences, one of which is most likely to be that we shall lose the respect and support of the rich, the powerful, and the privileged. So be it, if it has to be.

A decade and a half of ecumenism in Africa: problems, programmes, hopes

*Mercy Amba Oduyoye**

When I think of Dr. W.A. Visser 't Hooft, it is not so much of a staff person of the World Council of Churches as of the venerable old man of ecumenism, *Nana*, destined to join the "ancestors" of the ecumenical movement. A full-scale tribute to *Nana* would of course have to include a large number of organizations which have served as agents of the ecumenical movement. My main points of reference in this essay will be the All Africa Conference of Churches, the WCC, and the World Student Christian Federation. This personal offering is based on the firm conviction that, given the denominational way in which Christianity has been organized, ecumenism is a style to which one must be converted and committed. My own conversion to it came through the Student Christian Movement, and I have tried to work out that commitment through the WCC and the AACC.

The call to structured ecumenism based in Africa was issued by the International Missionary Council. The members of this overtly Euro-American institution, having introduced a divided Christianity into Africa and elsewhere, came to see that cooperation is better than competition; and at Accra in 1957/58 they accepted in principle the integration of the WCC and the IMC.[1] But if the swaddling clothes of this call to ecumenism were African, the baby itself was of uncertain parentage. Beneath the apparent unity displayed by Christian leaders in Africa lay a variety of sometimes conflicting purposes. For the Africans, cooperation at the local level was the highest priority; this assessment was not necessarily shared by the missionaries. Some persons were apprehensive about the emergence of an African Christian council not related either to the IMC or the WCC; others insisted that it was "the special responsibility of the IMC...to foster cooperation in the region and to inter-

---

* Ms MERCY A. ODUYOYE is teaching religious studies at Ibadan University, Nigeria. She is a member of the WCC's Central Committee.
1. R.K. Orchard, ed., *The Ghana Assembly of the IMC* (Edinburgh, 1958), p. 166.

pret the plan of integration and the nature and purpose of the two world bodies."[2]

In the atmosphere of the decision to integrate the IMC with the WCC, the All Africa Church Conference convened in Ibadan in January 1958. Fully a third of the membership of each conference was present at the other.[3] Even so, although the marriage between the WCC and the IMC in Africa was consummated, it seems to me that it was never a real union. Because the vow that "the two shall be one" was not taken with full seriousness, the child — the AACC — developed a sort of schizophrenia.

A strand of ecumenism in Africa which is often overlooked by European and American chroniclers, who tend to view Africa only from the North, and not as her sons and daughters see her, is the role played in its development by nationalism. The connection between the two emerges from remarks to the Accra conference delegates by Dr Kwame Nkrumah, then prime minister of Ghana. Paying tribute to the work that had been done by Western missionaries, Nkrumah noted that an independent Ghana was now engaged in the work of nation-building. Referring to the Christian message of Christmas, he asked how there could be goodwill "if Christians think more of their differences than of their wholehearted devotion to the God of all... You see Africa. You see the ambitions and hopes of millions of Africans....They need education...advancement...capital.... We see powerful peoples engaged in a futile and destructive armament race....What has this to do with the Christian charity proclaimed by the West?"[4]

Nkrumah's call, like that of other African leaders, was for political independence for Africa. This appeal coincided with the call for a more visible unity of Christians in Africa and greater self-determination for them. As colonies were to become nations, missions were to become churches. Indeed, the AACC and the Organization of African Unity may be seen as twins: a month before the IMC assembly, Nkrumah had hosted 62 nationalist organizations at the All-African Peoples Conference in Accra. Out of this had come the Organization of African Unity. Meetings — and even some consultations — of the AACC are received by African heads of state.[5] During every AACC assembly, several African heads of state as well as the OAU itself have sent greetings. Nor are these contacts mere formalities: African political leaders

---

2. *Ibid.*, p. 161.
3. *The Church in Changing Africa*. Report of the All Africa Church Conference, Ibadan, Jan. 1958, p. 5.
4. Orchard, *op. cit.*, pp. 148-50.
5. See *The Struggle Continues*. Report of the 3rd Assembly of the AACC, 1974.

of all faiths expect the Christian church to play a positive role in Africa. To neglect this expectation is to divorce the church from the realities of Africa.

The enduring goal of the ecumenical movement in Africa has always been to serve as a forum for the unfolding of Christianity in Africa. In his opening speech at Ibadan, Dr Francis Akanu Ibiam had given expression to this vision for the year ahead: "In the process of time we hope by the grace of God to achieve something which will bring all the churches in Africa together in our efforts to build up the great countries of this continent upon him."[6] To a large extent the agenda of African Christian leaders at Ibadan had corresponded with that of the missionary interests, but the two were not always to coincide. There were still many who were oriented to "saving the 'Dark Continent' from paganism," persons who would generate steam about polygamy while ignoring racism.

What is the nature of our partnership in mission with European and American Christians? This question, still unsolved, has been present from the beginning. Those who were surprised at Bangkok in 1972, when John Gatu, vice-chairman of the AACC general committee, called for Moratorium, had not been listening very carefully to the voices in the "younger" churches over the years. Already at Accra, the Asian call, "Send us not men, but money," had been reported by S.C. Graaf van Randwijck.[7] To put it candidly, when a similar appeal came from Africa, European and American "partners" were too ready to reply, "We cannot pay the piper unless we call the tune" — not, of course, in so many words, but this was certainly how some agencies acted. Money, personnel, and theological orientation were all packaged together and sent to Africa, bypassing the AACC and going directly to the daughter churches, often creating new structures in the process. (We shall pick up this facet of the problem later in the essay).

Already in 1958, Erik W. Nielsen commented, upon reading the IMC materials, that "there is as yet not nearly enough real Asian and African participation in our thinking."[8] From the beginning of the 19th century mission enterprise in Africa, the sentiment had been expressed that Africans should be trained to become evangelists to their own people. Societies working in Africa — more so than the missionaries — had proposed that Christians in Africa be constituted into self-governing, self-supporting, self-propagating churches. By 1958 it had become clear that it was time for all this to be taken

---

6. *The Church in Changing Africa*, pp. 9-10.
7. Orchard, *op. cit.*, p. 79.
8. *Ibid.*, p. 253.

seriously, for Africans — rather than white missionaries representing their societies — to form the predominant group at missionary council meetings. At the same time, Africans were coming into more leadership positions both in African councils and in the World Council of Churches. By the time *Nana* had left the staff of the WCC, the writing on the wall was clear: the time had come to let the children grow up. How effectively African leaders could function in these Euro-American structures was, of course, another matter.

In 1967 what must have been a bold step was taken: three Africans were employed at the WCC headquarters in Geneva. To be sure, some people could not yet tell the two women among them apart three years later! Yet I am convinced that the visibility of these three people together with three or four blacks from the United States and the Caribbean, contributed to the focus on racism which went to the General Assembly meeting at Uppsala in 1968 as part of the development emphasis.

I recall my own struggle during those years to find a suitable name for the churches that had resulted from the missionary ventures of European and American Christians in Africa. "Younger" or "newer" churches was one name often heard — but in that case what about the Ethiopian Orthodox Church? Some spoke of "daughter churches," but that term seemed appropriate only if it were made very clear that these were grown-up daughters. Whatever the designation, however, these churches were sending African delegates to conferences, and that created a situation in which those who contributed the finances were no longer the sole determinants of how the World Council of Churches moved.

Back home in Africa the AACC was engaged in a number of programmes designed to make the African churches more effective in their contributions to the development of Africa, the ecumenical movement, and the church at large. These were concrete steps directed at bringing to reality the hope expressed at the beginning of the AACC that (in Dr Ibiam's words) Africa might become "a continent from which emanate light, truth, and righteousness, knowledge, wisdom and understanding, goodness and prosperity, honour and blessing."[9] Structures, ideas, money, and people were of course needed. At Abidjan in 1969, the African churches had manifested a determination to develop their own personnel; in the meantime, European and American people continued to function in the AACC. The team of the Ecumenical Programme for Emergency Action in Africa (EPEAA), set up with a goal of $10,000,000, to help the refugee and development projects of the churches, had a black American as its director; there was another

---

9. *The Church in Changing Africa*, p. 10.

American on the programme, as well as a person from England and another from Germany, along with one Ghanaian — a typical ecumenical team of four (denominationally balanced) donors and one object of charity.[10] Africa was willing to accept this only so long as it helped to get on with the task of leadership development.

How relevant to the aspirations of the continent has all this ecumenically focused activity been? At Abidjan in 1969 the churches showed their determination to engage in the effort of the development of Africa. The oppression under which millions of African people suffer was recognized as the context in which the churches' mission is to be carried out. The churches of Europe and America had cooperated with the AACC in the salvage work with refugees; the pointed question now became, would they do the same in the fight against racist regimes in Southern Africa? Would they work side by side with liberation movements that were called Marxist and Communist?

By the time of the third assembly of the AACC in Lusaka in 1974, the African churches' response to the challenges facing them was a clear determination to support liberation movements seeking to rid Africa of white racist governments. Why should Christian action be limited to fire-brigade type rescue operations? Why restrict themselves to supporting refugees without having also endeavoured to tackle the social and economic and political factors that make people refugees?

But it was becoming evident that being tied to the apron-strings of European and American churches meant that African churches had to identify with the theological perspectives of those churches — and the ideological presuppositions and ethnocentricity that inevitably undergirded that theology. As AACC general secretary Burgess Carr put it, "Nothing exposes the weakness of the church in Africa more than the absence of a relevant theology to deal with the situation of injustice so rampant on our continent."[11]

The problems which had called for the EPEAA did not disappear when the five years of this programme came to an end. The churches themselves remained financially poor. Furthermore, the mere fact that there were more African names on the rosters of various commissions did not necessarily mean that the effective African presence was correspondingly increased, for in many cases their churches simply could not afford the airfare to send their delegates to meetings across the continent or in Europe. But the AACC had understood from the outset what effect its decision to show solidarity with

---

10. *AACC Bulletin*, June 1967, pp. 122-24.
11. *The Struggle Continues*, p. 78.

nationalist movements would have on financing from sources outside Africa. Nor was Burgess Carr's militant, radical, and hopeful vision of the role of the churches in Africa geared to maximize fund-raising from sources outside of Africa. Still, Lusaka's message to the churches of Africa had called on them "to allow Christ to set them free from easy dependence upon foreign money and men."[12] The churches were being summoned to self-reliance.

When Lusaka placed liberation, evangelism, self-reliance, and justice before the churches in Africa, it was also placing these issues before the church universal. How would the church face up to the challenges of the emergent socialist states? Having recognized the neo-colonialist economic pattern which keeps Africa on the periphery of the Western system, the churches had decided not to remain infantile, not to settle for the "fleshpots of Egypt," but to go out into the desert, not to emulate those African agents of multinational corporations and perform the "middleman" function for European and American theology in Africa. Living for Christ would surely mean dying to some material comforts.

The question of leadership remained an acute one after Lusaka. The calibre of African Christian leadership was too often determined through the World Council of Churches and through scholarship programmes funded by the mission boards. When theological education in Africa is funded in this way, the compass for its style and content is set elsewhere. This strategy of determining Africa's priorities from outside of Africa is the bane of the ecumenical movement on our continent — particularly since its intent is to thwart the forces of liberation and diminish the creative role of the AACC and WCC in Africa.

No discussion of the problems confronting ecumenism in Africa can overlook the reentry on the scene of "conservative evangelical" missions by way of some of the "indigenous" churches. (I prefer to call these *Aladura* churches — "praying churches" — since prayer is one of their most characteristic emphases.) One illustration of this movement was the effort of the International Congress of Christian Churches to hold its ninth congress in Nairobi in July 1975; its leader, the American fundamentalist radio preacher Carl McIntire, was allegedly deported by Kenyan authorities before the meeting could be held. Another case was the Pan-African Christian Leadership Assembly of December 1976. *Aladura* churches which have been infiltrated by this type of Christianity, as well as those created by the new missionary enterprise, are all actively anti-ecumenical, alleging that the World Council of Churches is Marxist and un-Christian and insufficiently

---

12. *Ibid.*, p. 74.

concerned with the evangelization of "pagan tribes." A real problem is that the money behind PACLA is said to be coming from the very mission boards that have seen fit to suspend support to the AACC, claiming that the AACC is no longer interested in issues of evangelism and the Bible. The result is a resurgence of denominationalism in Africa through the confessional families.

In this connection, I think Ulrich Duchrow's sentiments about the World Confessional Families can be applied very pointedly to the African situation.[13] "Bilateral doctrinal discussions," the "structural system which takes as its basis the confessional formation of the ecumenical movement," and the divisiveness and isolationism and direct control embedded in bilateral aid constitute a clear threat to the ecumenical movement in Africa in particular. In a sense the World Confessional Families are but the religious version of the commercial multinational corporations: Those who hold the largest number of shares make the big decisions. The World Council of Churches' ideal of conciliar community is being constantly undermined by these advocates of "multinational denominations." Churches in the cities and villages of Africa do not have to exert much effort to have ecumenical services. The mass revival-type of evangelism cuts across the denominations, and there are joint efforts to keep religious freedom as a live option in Africa.

These are some of the problems which challenge our programmes and hopes for the growth of ecumenism in Africa. There have also been some programmes which, in the face of obstacles like these, seem to me to have been seminal. Unfortunately, issues related to Africa usually come very late to the agenda of implementation in international ecumenical bodies. One reason for this is Africa's preferred style of oral presentation, which places it at an immediate disadvantage in an arena where written reports and memoranda attract the primary attention.

Yet there have been conferences in which African leadership has been raised up or existing leadership brought into the limelight. The statesmanlike contributions of S.H. Ammisah, which built up the AACC and managed to keep a balance between the well-being of Africa and the interests of the Euro-American churches, was appreciated through several meetings. In the Conference on Church and Society, Mondlane, Igo, Adegbola, and Carr featured prominently; more importantly, this event insured that Christianity in Africa would never again be used as an opium to get people to accept something less than "life abundant."

---

13. These ideas are developed in his book, *Konflikt um die Oekumene: Christusbekenntnis — in welcher Gestalt der ökumenischen Bewegung?* (Munich: Chr. Kaiser, 1980).

Development discussions were at their most intensive in 1967, when I joined the Youth Department of the World Council of Churches. It was at a staff meeting in the Ecumenical Centre that I first heard the term "enlightened self-interest" during a discussion of the source of the church's concern for development — and it was in a contribution from *Nana* himself. I have never forgotten that. Uppsala's development interest, and the Abidjan emphasis on the same, did much to raise the awareness of people — Christians and others — about the real agenda of the world, the locus of God's saving activity, and the responsibility of the church.

As a prophetic voice, the AACC has served Africa well. As a reconciling movement, its role in the Sudan and the oil it poured on the troubled waters of Nigeria (so insensitively stirred up by the WCC in Uppsala) have been crucial. At other levels, too, some basic accomplishments have been registered. The village polytechnics begun by the National Christian Council of Kenya and the Malawi Rural Improvement Programme illustrate development efforts, while the Urban-Industrial Mission at Tema symbolizes a determination to be relevant in changing Africa. More recently, regionalization became a reality in the World Student Christian Federation, and work was undertaken in close cooperation with the AACC, particularly in educational programmes for young people. The All-Africa Youth and Student Conference, jointly sponsored by the WSCF and the AACC in 1969, was to the 1970s what Nairobi 1962 was to the 1960s.

But for me it is the Programme to Combat Racism which is the core of our involvement for the past fifteen years. All the pronouncements which the WCC has issued concerning racism since 1948 have to be verified, justified, and put into practice. The link between economic development and white racism has been confirmed. An AACC research project has established Western collaboration with South Africa in the development of nuclear power. Of course, there are numerous other facets to the PCR. My hope is that its active stance will not break the back of the ecumenical movement as symbolized by Geneva.

Let me conclude by rephrasing what Dr Ibiam said at the inception of the ecumenical movement in Africa. We do not need ecclesiastical marionettes, nor do we have any use for Christianity that is a tranquillizer rather than a stimulant. In the last analysis, it is in the interest of all who call themselves Christians and believe that God is at work in the world to struggle not only for the survival of ecumenism, but also for a glimpse of the kingdom through it. May the work of God begun by our "ancestors" never cease until the earth is filled with the glory of God, as the waters cover the seas.

The "gadfly" on trial:
the "political" commitment
of the World Council of Churches

Alexandros Papaderos*

And so, men of Athens, I am now making my defence not for my own sake, as one might imagine, but far more for yours, that you may not by condemning me err in your treatment of the gift God gave you. For if you put me to death, you will not easily find another, who, to use a rather absurd figure, attaches himself to the city as a gadfly to a horse, which, though large and well bred, is sluggish on account of his size and needs to be aroused by stinging. I think the god fastened me upon the city in some such capacity, and I go about arousing, and urging and reproaching each one of you, constantly alighting upon you everywhere the whole day long. Such another is not likely to come to you, gentlemen; but if you take my advice, you will spare me. But you, perhaps, might be angry, like people awakened from a nap, and might slap me, as Anytos advises, and easily kill me; then you would pass the rest of your lives in slumber, unless God, in his care for you, should send someone to sting you.[1]

When I was invited to provide an Orthodox comment on the "political" commitment of the World Council of Churches for this festschrift, I immediately recalled this moving and prophetic passage from Plato. Thereafter, it pursued *me* as a "gadfly," leading me to concentrate on the "gadfly" role of the ecumenical movement in general and the World Council of Churches in particular. Though I can only guess at the *daimonion* which possessed the pioneers of the modern ecumenical movement, I am convinced that we should have had neither an ecumenical movement nor a World Council of Churches if these pioneers had not been provided as heaven-sent "gadflies" to arouse the churches, spur them, reprove them — and certainly to trouble them too!

---

* Dr. ALEXANDROS PAPADEROS is Director of the Orthodox Academy of Crete.
1. From Plato, *Apology*, 18, tr. H. N. Fowler (Loeb Classical Library) (Cambridge, Mass., 1966), pp. 111-13.

This is especially true of the man to whom this volume is dedicated. May he continue to be the *Batouchka*, the spiritual leader, the "little father" that the Russian Orthodox long ago saw him to be.[2] Willem A. Visser 't Hooft will certainly be remembered by the church as the most persistent "gadfly" of world Christianity in the twentieth century.

But the World Council of Churches, which he laboriously constructed with prophetic devotion, has for some years been on trial. Socrates, who already "lived with the Logos" long before the incarnation of the Logos,[3] was accused of "atheism"; he did indeed preach "new *daimonia*" — truths which astonished the "pious" and gave them offense, "words which, like bees, sting and perish in stinging" (in the phrase of Odysseas Elytis, *To Axion Esti*); words which lead the one who utters them to his death. The dangerous truths and stinging words of the ecumenical movement, forced on the attention of contemporary churches and Christians by the World Council of Churches, often have the same effect as the mordant bites of the gadfly. It was obviously too much to expect Anytos — Socrates' chief accuser — to ignore such a disturbance of his slumbers. The critics therefore assumed the task of the *diabolos* and incited the Athenians to initiate a prosecution in order to get the insect out of the way before it was too late. The trial had already lasted a few years. The judges, the accusers, and the charges change from time to time; but the trial itself still continues, sometimes amid great tensions, sometimes in a lower key, while additional incriminatory evidence is awaited.

It is understandable that Orthodoxy should take part in this trial, for the ecumenical gadfly has made itself felt in a quite special degree in our body as well. It is certainly no exaggeration to say that, second only to the predominance of an atheistic system of government in many Orthodox countries, the ecumenical movement represents the major challenge to Orthodoxy in this century. For although we should not minimize Orthodoxy's own contribution to the creation of the ecumenical movement — indeed, to the claim of the movement to be called ecumenical at all — it nevertheless constitutes the first massive challenge of Protestantism to Orthodox Christianity. This is so above all because of the more or less dominant presence of the Reforma-

---

2. Cf. W.A. Visser 't Hooft, *Memoirs* (London, 1973), p. 271.
3. In the words of Justin Martyr: "We have been taught that Christ was First-begotten of God (the Father) and we have indicated above that he is the Word of whom *all mankind* partakes. Those who lived by reason are Christians, even though they have been considered atheists: such as, among the Greeks, Socrates, Heraclitus, and others like them." Tr. by T.B. Falls, in *The Fathers of the Church: A New Translation. The Writings of St. Justin Martyr* (Washington, 1948), p. 83.

tion churches in the ecumenical movement from the very beginning and the likelihood that this dominant presence will continue in the foreseeable future. Both theologically and in socio-political terms, this represents a permanent challenge for Orthodoxy.

But the Orthodox position on the socio-political commitment of the World Council of Churches is not and cannot indeed be a uniform one. So far, Orthodoxy has offered only partial answers. Nor can a pan-Orthodox answer on the basis of common reflections be expected in the near future, unless the projected Great and Holy Synod were to meet soon and also be able to discuss this important question (as is the intention). Even then, the answer could not be complete and final, since the challenge itself is not uniform or unalterable. What Orthodoxy perceives in its encounter with Protestantism in the setting of the ecumenical movement is a polyphony which is not always in harmony.

But it is not only this polyphony, further reinforced by global political and cultural tensions, which makes any uniform response by Orthodoxy impossible. It is even difficult for Orthodoxy itself to achieve a harmonious symphony on the contemporary social and political field. The context in which Orthodoxy lives today is marked by an extremely diverse pluralism, permitting only a polyphonic expression of the self-awareness and world-outlook of the Orthodox Christian, which were once more or less uniform.[4] It is only to be hoped that among these many sounds the inner harmony of the Orthodox ethos can be maintained. To give an answer, based on this Orthodox ethos, to the socio-political challenge of the ecumenical movement and above all of the present world situation is a long overdue Orthodox responsibility. Recent steps in this direction have unfortunately been very few, though encouraging in themselves.[5] To a certain extent these constitute a solid starting point.

---

4. Cf. A. Papaderos, "Das liturgische Selbst- und Weltbewusstsein des byzantinischen Menschen," in *Kyros*, IV, No. 3 (1964), 206ff.

5. In addition to the Pan-Orthodox Conferences, which have been held since 1961, and the 2nd Pan-Orthodox Conference of Theologians (Athens, 1976; cf. *Procès-Verbaux du Deuxième Congrès de Théologie Orthodoxe*, Athens, 1978), we should mention two consultations documented in C. Patelos, ed., *The Orthodox Church in the Ecumenical Movement* (Geneva, 1978) — those on "Confessing Christ Today" (Rumania, 1974) and on "The Church's Struggle for Justice and Unity" (Crete, 1975); also the 1977 Valamo Consultation on "The Ecumenical nature of the Orthodox Witness," published as a paper by the WCC Orthodox Task Force; and the 1978 consultation in Crete on "Church and Service: The Orthodox Approach to Diaconia," from which my paper "Liturgische Diakonie" has been published as a manuscript (Otterbach, 1979).

Comfort and pleasure?

In every court case the first question is the identity of the accused. He must say himself who he is before the case can begin, before the prosecutor and defense counsel can begin to outline their own picture. What the World Council of Churches is intended to be has been discussed, decided, and formulated by the member churches together in statements and agreements. But what has this produced? How does the World Council of Churches really view itself?

Let me focus first on a characteristic statement. When Eugene Carson Blake welcomed the Ecumenical Patriarch Athenagoras to the Geneva headquarters of the WCC on November 6, 1967, he compared the World Council of Churches to a building created by the churches for "pleasure" and "use." But this building was still far from completion. More rooms would be required as the ecumenical family grew. Thus the plans had to be changed constantly in order to ensure greater "pleasure" and "usefulness!"[6] Dr Blake's metaphor would have given the false impression that the WCC's main task is to offer the member churches pleasure and comfort, if he had not concluded by referring to the danger a building brings with it — that of its occupants' settling down in peaceful isolation. I am convinced that not a few Christians, perhaps even many member churches, look to the Council more for pleasure and comfort than for stings from the gadfly. Were the Council itself to endorse this expectation, it would certainly have failed in one of its major tasks, that of being "a continuous constructive challenge to the churches," as Metropolitan Meliton of Chalcedon said in a commentary on the Uppsala Assembly.[7] In view of this danger, it seems appropriate here to address to the World Council of Churches some questions raised by the passage from Plato.

— For whose sake does the WCC in each specific case defend itself in this continuing trial? For its own sake or for the sake of the "Athenians?"

— Does the WCC still regard itself as a gift of God to Christendom, and does it recognize that this gift is not an end in itself, nor is its purpose some goal chosen by the Council itself, but really only these "Athenians" themselves, even when they come forward as its accusers?

— Has it really been the conviction of the WCC — to which it still cleaves — that it does have its own quite specific task to fulfil and that it has therefore been given by God "to the city as a gadfly?"

— Does it continue to sting the large horse which is prone to sluggishness, even to be a deliberate nuisance to it? Or has it become so alarmed by the

---

6. Cf. Patelos, *op. cit.*, pp. 251ff.
7. *Ibid.*, p. 294.

horse's reactions that it now strikes it gently, even at the risk of sending it into deeper slumber? Does it not sometimes even seem inclined to imagine itself transformed into a noble steed and to accept laziness as its proper station in life?

— How acute is the danger for the "Athenians" themselves? Will they continue thankfully to support the WCC, instead of condemning it? Or, following Anytos, will they become morose and frivolously condemn it, destroy it so they can be free to sleep on with untroubled conscience?

The World Council of Churches and the temptation of power

The tempting of the saints by power is a permanent challenge in Christian life, from which not even the World Council of Churches is exempt. For in its dealings with power, it is always in danger — whether it is powerful or powerless — of acting in such a way that power actually tempts it. It can either come under the thumb of those who possess power in this world, or, because of its own concentration of power, come to trust in power and to adopt in its own thinking and action the attitude of the powerful.

In the first place, the Council can fall victim to power structures within the ecumenical fellowship itself. Those member churches which dispose of wealth in one form or other (wealth of tradition, or spirituality, or revolutionary zeal, or missionary experience, or money, or relief service, or connections with economic interests; or even member churches under pressure from ideological or military blocs) may perhaps be tempted to get their own way and seek to manipulate the WCC in the direction they choose. The World Council, it is then said, must have a more "vertical," less "horizontal" orientation; it should be more conservative or more eager for revolution, less "profane," more "spiritual," "more cautious" or "more courageous," ideologically neutral or ideologically committed, against militarism, of course, but careful not to risk jobs in the arms industries; it should resolutely seek peace, yet, for all that, not underestimate the need for the balance of terror ... and so on and so on!

The World Council, moreover, is not exempt from the danger which confronts us all, namely, that of being confronted by the powerful of this world in such a way that these can commit us as Christians and churches to their own policies and in their own interests, forcing us into an alliance with them or at least ensuring themselves of our silence by intimidating us or turning us into helpless robots serving their ends.

But it seems to me that the real danger facing the World Council in relation to power lies in its own self-awareness. For we need no reminder how strong the original diabolical temptation remains, whispering to us that we might be something different — indeed something more — and tempting us to break out of our real existence as defined. I have already referred to the danger of the Council's one day yielding to the temptation to be no longer a mere gadfly and to become instead a noble steed! I am not referring here primarily to the desire sometimes attributed to the Council of becoming a super church. Many of the earlier suspicions of this seem to have been dispelled. I am referring, rather, to the charge that the Council overestimates itself and gives the impression that it is really in a position to penetrate the contemporary power structures of politics, militarism, economics, technology, science, racism, sexism, exploitation, ideological controversy, and the mass media, and to bring about an effective change in their substance or direction.

The frantic way some member churches — and even non-church circles — react favourably or unfavourably to this or that social or political initiative of the World Council gives the impression that they believe it is really in a position to realize what is hoped for or to avoid what is feared in each case. If the World Council of Churches itself were to come to believe this, it would mean, as I see it, that the Council had completely misunderstood the essence of its socio-political task: namely, that of being simply a gadfly, a voice in the wilderness, a sign of hope, a signpost to him who alone is the way from the hopelessness of our human situation.[8] The WCC would then also have failed to accomplish another important task of the ecumenical movement, that of offering the churches the possibility of exchanging their experiences in their dealings with power in the past and today, in the hope that this or that church might thereby be delivered more easily from its own dreams of power and recognize where its real power lies, in the foolishness of the cross! In its gadfly role, at any rate, the WCC, for all its powerlessness, will never be able to abandon the difficult task of challenging — as the crucified Christ did — the principalities and powers (sometimes even the "spiritual" principalities and powers) of this world.

Masking and unmasking

A few years ago, in the Greece of the "Colonels" a sermon by Metropolitan Meliton of Chalcedon was broadcast over the radio. The sermon, preached at the beginning of Lent, provoked considerable excitement. It was a hymn in praise of the carnival, in praise of masks. These masks allow us, at least once a year, to appear in public without hesitation as the people we really are all the time. On this day we are not afraid to wear our "face" in

---

8. Cf. W.A. Visser 't Hooft, *No Other Name: The Choice Between Syncretism and Christian Universalism* (London, 1963).

public, whereas the rest of the year we are compelled to live and suffer in the fear of being unmasked.

I often wonder whether the fear the WCC awakens in some of us cannot in part be traced back to the fact that it is constantly confronting us with decisions which have the same effect on us as an unmasking. For making believe, pretending to be, is certainly one of our favourite habits. How often we resist the question, "What are you really like?" But this question is constantly being addressed to us in the ecumenical fellowship, whenever we are faced with concrete problems and tasks which shake our normal assumptions and behaviour and force us to put our cards on the table. At the Eighth Assembly of the Conference of European Churches in Crete in 1979, when the message of welcome from the Ecumenical Patriarch Dimitrios officially urged the Roman Catholic Church to become a full member of the Conference,[9] embarrassment seemed to run like an electric current through the assembly hall. Everyone suddenly realized that this specific invitation acted as a touchstone for ecumenical honesty and maturity on all sides.

We can all recall similar and even more critical moments of ecumenical unmasking, however limited our ecumenical experience may be. For example, some have not rested content with mere phrases about human rights, racism, minorities, refugees, but have been prepared to uncover, unmask, the whole complex of root causes of such evils. Even when we reject some particular WCC venture into the social and political realm, indeed, precisely *because* we reject it, we are drawn into a process of inner tension. We find ourselves called upon not only to justify ourselves to others but also to question our own real grounds for repudiating this venture. Here, too, we can find ourselves unmasked. However painful the stings of conscience resulting from direct confrontation with concrete realities may be, we should surely be grateful to the ecumenical movement for this special ministry — all the more so since it is impossible to say for sure which is the more painful, the unmasking of our own face or the unmasking of our brother's. In either case, the pain caused is a healing one, especially perhaps when it exposes our assimilation to the powers and structures of this world and makes us aware of our powerlessness, in the isolation of our dividedness, effectively to fulfil the prophetic ministry entrusted to us.

The stinging "thou"

Strictly speaking, it is not the World Council of Churches itself which performs the gadfly role, but the confrontation which it brings about between

---

9. For the full text see the report of the assembly, *Unity in the Spirit — Diversity in the Churches*, pp. 50f.

the churches, and with facts which challenge, arouse, and stimulate them, just as gadflies become obtrusive and persistent. In the initial phase of the ecumenical era, this was precisely the effect of the mere encounter of the churches with one another. Suddenly representatives of churches founded by the apostles had to sit down at the same table with "young" churches, venerable patriarchs with lay theologians, even with women, and act with them on an equal footing, sometimes having even to be content with secondary positions and silently to put up with public marginalization. On the other hand, Christians keen for reform had to exercise patience with a ponderous and imposing ritual.

Again, representatives of nations which had recently clashed in war met together while the wounds were still unhealed, hearts were still heavy with guilt, bitterness, suspicion, or even perhaps illusory victory. Centuries-old assumptions clashed with each other and were shaken; firm convictions were called in question. At every turn, people were confronted with differences all the more stinging because of their mutual claims to validity: different religious experiences, different ways of thinking and arguing about theology, different views as to the tasks of the church, different individual and church life-styles. All these were painful stings for everyone concerned, and they were able to bear them patiently and experience them as creative spurs prodding them forward only because they were sincerely searching for fellowship and unity in the power of the Holy Spirit.

Stinging facts

As I have said, confronting the church with facts is the second way the World Council of Churches has to perform its role as gadfly. It is not always clear, here, what the "rock of offense" really is in each particular case. Is it the way the WCC acts or what it actually does? Is it really the way grants from the Special Fund of the Programme to Combat Racism are allocated that provokes the notorious controversy, or is it perhaps the fear that as a result of this grant a given church may find itself in conflict with forces and vested interests in its own milieu which depend on the continuance of the *status quo*? In either case, this or that church is made to feel the sting of facts, especially in the case of programmes with a direct political relevance. The special element in this context is of course that the "facts" we are confronted with no longer relate exclusively to our immediate area of mission but embrace distant areas and situations which are not so easy for us to understand. For one of the great blessings conferred on the churches by the ecumenical movement is the way it has helped them to come out of their isolation and provincialism and to encounter world Christendom. Since all of us are constantly tempted to think and act in this way, the World Council of Churches is surely indispensable to the churches here in its role as a "gadfly." All the more so in view of the fact that, despite the enrichment of our macrodimensional experience of ecumenism and world politics, we are always tempted to cling instead to our microdimensional habits.[10]

Indolent silence

All of us are constantly being summoned to account not only for our speaking but also for our silences. The indolence which inclines us to silence is another of those church habits from which the World Council of Churches should help to free us by its gadfly stings. Certainly there is a silence which is holy. The Christian mystics, like the mystics of all religions and like Christian piety generally, are familiar with the sense of the *mysterium tremendum*, that dread mystery before which one can only keep silence in reverence and astonishment.[11] In complete contrast to this however, there is a sinful and guilty silence often cultivated by those of us whose business it is to speak, especially those of us who have to speak up for those who must remain silent. If it is a virtue to remain silent when injustice is done to us, it is certainly a sin not to speak when the unjustly treated are before our eyes. The silence which is the fruit of fear, of lack of love and courage, or even a tactic dictated by self-interest is certainly not the silence approved by God.

Here once again we have to acknowledge the sluggishness of the horse, the most ancient and the most modern tendency of the people of God and its leaders. The whole history of salvation, Old Testament and New, is surely characterized by that all-too-familiar and matter-of-course apathy of silence; so much so, indeed, that prophecy, the protest against silence, seems almost a mere pause for thought before a correction of course. And yet we know that God never leaves his church for long without the gadflies, without those "fools," those prophets and martyrs who even in our day raise their voices and let the world know "that all these things — these concessions, this docility, these compromises, as well as the traditional truces between the Church and the earthly powers — are evil."[12]

Nevertheless, although we know that the *orge* — the wrath — of God hangs over us when we ignore the prophets and despise prophecy, we go on

---

10. On the problem of our micro- and macro-dimensional tasks, see my "Liturgische Diakonie," pp. 11, 21f.

11. This is the terminology first used by R. Otto, *The Idea of the Holy* (London, 1926).

12. Quoted from A. Solzhenitsyn, *Kirche und Politik*, ed. P. Ingold and I. Rakosa (Zürich, 1973), pp. 68f.

doing so again and again, preferring silence to speaking at the right time and place and in the right way. It must be recognized and humbly confessed that even Orthodoxy is no exception to this rule, despite the great host of its fathers and saints of old and of today who, because they have spoken when "sensible" people were keeping quiet, have suffered torture and martyrdom. I am not referring here to the conduct of our spiritual leaders during the long period of alien rule over our Orthodox peoples, for in this respect the church has again and again proved to be the pioneer of liberation. Nor am I referring to the "symphony" between Church and State, which is not always correctly understood by our Western brothers and sisters. I am referring principally to the way the misuse of this "symphony" has been tolerated, its reduction to a usurpatory "monophony" on the part of the State, deliberate cooperation in the "reconciliation" of contradictory data, the closing of our eyes and ears to crying social injustice, our indolent persistence with familiar platitudes so that the *kairos* passed us by and did not return.

Partisanship or neutrality

Finally, a brief discussion of the problem of neutrality is appropriate, since it is often used to excuse our indolence.

The criticism levelled at the WCC is usually not directed against its social and political commitment as such. In principle, there seems to be general agreement that the World Council of Churches has social and political tasks to fulfil, especially since the member churches can hardly oppose what they themselves are already doing (though some of them occasionally level charges at the WCC which could easily be turned back on themselves; cf. Rom. 2:1). Certainly no one wants the Christian family represented in the ecumenical movement to lag behind what even the Roman Catholic Church and many Christian and secular organizations are doing in the social and political field. For the World Council of Churches has a long history of pioneering work in this field. Quite apart from that, the member churches would also be guilty of inconsistency if they wished to prevent the Council from carrying out social and political tasks which they themselves have entrusted to it. The attacks so often made, therefore, are not on the social and political commitment as such but rather on its *status* and its *direction*.

It is asserted, in the first place, that the social and political commitment is increasingly being given too high a status among the activities of the Council. The question which needs to be asked is whether it really is a case of *too much* social and political commitment. By what standard is this judged? Can it possibly be the actual distress of a world tortured by famine, injustice, and exploitation? Or the measure of the evil to be mastered, along with all its labyrinthine dehumanizing structures? It would certainly be impossible to measure the work of the WCC against all that. Such a comparison would certainly cut it down to size. More important still, it would be absurd if it were to give the impression that the Council is already so gripped by the temptation to power as really to believe it has the power or the assignment to rid the world of all this evil!

No matter how much some enthusiasts and social ideologues may occasionally try to sidetrack this or that debate in that direction, those who hold responsible positions in the Council are surely remote from any such temptation. Obviously, therefore, the criterion is not *too much* social and political commitment, but *too little*, that is, too little promotion of the goals which some member churches have seen from the very beginning as the *real* tasks of the Council, which alone justify its existence. According to some critics, these goals, which focus on concern for the spiritual renewal of the church and efforts for its unity, have been increasingly neglected if not laid aside completely.

Here I cannot dwell on this in any detail or offer even a provisional reckoning of previous efforts to achieve theological agreement and visible, tangible unity. It is not easy to recognize advances in this area, much less to measure them statistically. They are not sensational news for the daily press and make no direct impact on the wider public. But the question is how far we have to seek our unity first and foremost in theological reflection and sacramental fellowship or need to test, recognize, and experience it also at the same time in our confrontation with the social and political challenges of our time.

It was not by chance that, in the famous 1920 Encyclical of the Ecumenical Patriarchate, priority should have been given to the joint fulfilment of "practical" tasks by the churches. What prompted this was not simply a recognition of the risk of starting out ecumenical rapprochement with theological discussions. Nor can the recommended preference for what today is called "horizontalism" be adequately explained by the post-war situation in 1920. In addition to these factors there was undoubtedly also the conviction that shared commitment on behalf of humanity in Christ's name would also make it easier to recognize unity and strive for it.

Today, after all the experiences we have been through together, we should ask ourselves: How far is it true to say that there really has been a shift of the priorities of the World Council of Churches in the direction of social and political commitment? And if there has been such a shift, we must ask how far social and political commitment can promote the cause of unity or injure it.

It would require a detailed survey of the entire history of the ecumenical movement to answer the first of these questions. On the whole, however, I think it would be fair to say that, if there *has* been any shift in the priorities of the World Council of Churches, it has been in the opposite direction to that which is usually assumed, namely, *at the expense of social commitment rather than to its advantage.* The basis for this bold assertion is the fact that ecumenical reflection and cooperation originated above all in the desire that the churches should respond effectively to crying social needs, and the fact that many of these needs were to some extent met with an astonishing vigour and an exemplary commitment of persons and resources under the ecumenical banner, both in the period before the Second World War as well as immediately following it. But this commitment, with its primary focus on the relief of need, also produced at the same time the great turning point in the quest for unity. Would anyone seriously argue that theological discussions, however skilled and intensive, could ever have achieved even a fraction of what was immediately achieved in the advancement of Christian unity by that total Christian commitment? For example, in dispelling mutual ignorance and a whole range of prejudices, in breaking down barriers, in bringing to light the diversity of God's gifts to his people, in renewing the congregations, but also in engendering fresh theological thinking on ecclesiological, anthropological, ethical, and social issues, not only discussed interconfessionally for the first time but also grasped and experienced existentially at the level of personal relationships. Certainly an equivalent commitment with similar positive effects on the ecumenical climate and the advancement of unity has no longer been evident in recent years.

As for the question of the direction of ecumenical social and political commitment, there has undoubtedly been a shift. But this shift seems to me qualitative rather than quantitative. It is not a question of "more" or "less" but rather of the *objective* of what is striven for and done. This shift goes hand in hand with a *changed understanding of mission* in recent world missionary conferences (Mexico City 1963, Bangkok 1972/1973, and more recently still Melbourne 1980), in which the wholeness of the human being has become more and more the focus of interest, and which reaffirms the indivisibility of salvation and human well-being and emphasizes the relevance of the kingdom of God for this world here and now.

Direction here means *partisanship*, a daring and perhaps even dangerous tendency of the World Council of Churches (as is often asserted). This is clearly the old and still unsolved problem of the justified or unjustified *neutrality* of the Christian commitment. Some persons overlook the inherent contradiction between these two concepts: commitment necessarily implies a rejection of neutrality. It was thought once that neutrality pointed in no particular direction. Thus the thing to do in the work of the Christian academies, for example, was to provide a neutral forum for encounter and controversy, hoping that truth would emerge triumphant. But even this view has been shaken. It has been realized that neutrality of this kind only appears to be above the parties, whereas in fact it is extremely partisan, since it allows the *status quo* to appear to be just as legitimate as every new alternative striven for on the basis of Christian commitment.

Meanwhile, thanks to the social and political commitment of the World Council of Churches, and the theology developed as a result of wrestling with this commitment, many of us have come to see that the eschatological Exodus initiated in Jesus was a clear rejection of the *status quo* and that his gospel counts for those who count for nothing. It is directed to all human beings who are "poor," that is, who are ready to become poor, who are willing not to "purchase" the grace of God with what they have and are but to receive God's love and deliverance in complete solidarity with those who have nothing and are nothing.

Those who have much and therefore think they are something have some quite understandable difficulty with the biblical passages now emphasized: Jesus became poor, not rich (2 Cor. 9:9); he identified himself with the cause of the poor, not with that of the rich (Matt. 25:21f.); the kingdom of God is promised to the poor, not to the rich (Matt. 5:3; James 2:5).

But these difficulties can only be surmounted by those who are willing in the end to understand that where Christ makes himself known to them they will not be dealing with a pallid ethics of "love of the neighbour" but with the basic ontological categories of ecclesiology, as epitomized in the principle *ubi Christus, ibi Ecclesia*. This elementary truth exposes the absurdity of any expectation that the unity of the church can either be maintained or restored by observing strict neutrality towards social and political controversy. By the very attachment of our church tradition to space and time, by the pressures of the social and political conditions in which we have to live, and by our own personal lives, we already belong to a "party," we already takes sides (wittingly or unwittingly), we are already subject to the party line and used or even misused by the party. It hardly seems possible for us any longer, therefore, to understand, strive for, and achieve — that is, be able to experience — our unity as a socio-political "symphony" as well. *"The goal is not a fellowship exempt from conflict but one which is reconciled by*

God."[13] This statement by the Council of the Evangelical Church in Germany points in the only possible direction in which we can all confidently strive.

We have here a primary task which all of us must seek to carry out at all levels, from the congregations to the supreme courts of the church, as well as in our dialogue with people of different experiences, religions, cultures, and ideologies. On the way towards this "fellowship in controversy," reconciled by God and with God, we shall perhaps also recognize it as our specific Christian mission to help to change, and so to reconcile, the forces which are the source of conflicts today between people and nations. The criterion by which the member churches should judge the pioneer programmes which the World Council of Churches is commissioned by its decision-making bodies to carry out, and the initiatives it takes, and even perhaps its seemingly utopian models of a future world order ought not simply to be the likelihood of their achievement or their potential for complicating the relationships of this or that church with the state or industry. Their essential and most valuable function is a "signalling" one. They are signposts which may perhaps also have the effect of a "gadfly" sting, prodding the life of our churches awake when we are tempted as we usually are to remain in our indolence.

Those who dissociate themselves from these contemporary tasks of Christendom will hardly be in a position to excuse themselves by pretending that the work of the ecumenical movement in general and that of the World Council of Churches in particular has not provided us with the requisite equipment for these tasks: mature theological and socio-political insights, an extensive and varied ecumenical body of material, instrumental and other resources for the work of ecumenical education, and, above all, a network unprecedented in the history of Christianity of global communication and cooperation, in the solidarity of a fellowship of brothers and sisters which has certainly been to a large extent sensitized by the sting of the ecumenical gadfly.

---

13. "Memorandum on the Relationship of the EKD to the WCC," *Ökumenische Rundschau*, XXVIII, Part 1 (Jan. 1979), p. 43.

Ecumenism in Asia: an assessment

M. M. Thomas*

Ecumenical goals for Asia ...

The ecumenical vision of Visser 't Hooft for the Asian churches was spelled out on various occasions, especially in his 1959 John R. Mott Lectures, delivered in Kuala Lumpur at the inauguration of the East Asia Christian Conference (now the Christian Conference of Asia).[1] The characteristic clarity and depth of his vision make these lectures impressive even after two decades, and an assessment of ecumenism in Asia in 1980 can best be made in the light of what Visser 't Hooft put forth then as goals of Asian ecumenism. He stressed three points.

First, ecumenism is churches in mutual dialogue in Christ. Asian ecumenism should be understood essentially as the conversation of the churches of Asia among themselves and with the non-Asian churches in Christ. This inter-church dialogue is necessary for mutual correction and for a common discrimination of the Word of God from human words. It will lead each participating church to an increasingly deeper conversation with Jesus Christ, and all the churches to a fuller knowledge of Jesus Christ as their one "common foundation" and "common criterion of truth." It will help "purify our message and our task" and discover "a common word for the Church and the world" in our time.

Second, ecumenism is liberation of the churches from an idolatrous attachment to outdated values and patterns of life which are passing away. For Asia it means freeing the churches from the legacy of Western Christendom, which was transferred to Asia in the period of Western expansion inaugurated by Vasco da Gama. The end of these patterns in the relationship of church to state, society, culture, and religions must become the hour of spiritual liberation of the Asian churches from the idols of

---

* Dr. M. M. Thomas, a former Moderator of the WCC's Central Committee, was Director of the Christian Institute for the Study of Religion and Society in Bangalore, India, until his retirement.
1. Published as *A Decisive Hour for the Christian Mission* (London, 1960), pp. 46-71.

that epoch. In Visser 't Hooft's words the Vasco da Gama epoch was a cause of weakness, embodying "the Church in a framework which could easily become a prison." Now was the hour when the church could rediscover how it depends only on God, enabling it to carry on its mission in greater purity and without entangling alliances. This spiritual liberation is the path towards ecumenism. "Churches imprisoned in cultural and social patterns can hardly be ecumenical; on the other hand, churches which stand on their feet naturally seek to establish fellowship with each other." This is the proper setting and the content of ecumenical dialogue among the Asian churches and beween them and other churches in the ecumenical movement.

Third, this spiritual liberation *from* the bygone world and its idols is liberation *for* a new Christ-centred involvement in the emerging Asian world, with a view to its renewal in Christ. In the Bible, freedom in Christ is to "be available for the work of Christ in the world." This can neither be withdrawal from nor idolatrous conformity and syncretism with the new Asian world; it involves "real conversation" with that world of independent nationhood, renewing societies, renascent indigenous cultures, and resurgent religions, in order to witness to Christ. Visser 't Hooft spells out several specific Asian issues and goals, and some of these deserve special mention here.

1. *The communication of the gospel of Christ and reinterpretation of Christianity in terms of the categories of Asian cultures, religions, and life.* If the Asian churches are to avoid both becoming "introverted communities which seek to defend themselves" and idolatrous syncretism with life around, "this task of reinterpretation of Christianity must be undertaken. For as long as Christianity is understood by many as a *Western* religion because it has come so largely in a Western form of expression, it cannot be made fully clear that at its heart there is the universal and absolute claim of the Lord Jesus Christ upon *all* men." This reinterpretation of an Asian Christianity is significant for the Western churches too: "mutual correction is one of the great functions of the ecumenical movement."

2. *The search for church union.* The framework for church unity must be "common theological insights" which transcend and comprehend the different confessional traditions in "a wider and deeper affirmation of Christian truth." Church unity must transcend and overcome not merely confessional and doctrinal differences but also the tribal, linguistic, ethnic, and racial identities and divisions in which the churches are embedded.

3. *The struggle for "the responsible society" as "witness to the Lordship of Christ over the world."* Today the question is: Have the Asian churches moved in this direction?

An assessment

The writings I come across these days in the forums of the Christian Conference of Asia and the national councils of churches of the various Asian countries would seem to suggest a negative answer to this question. Two recent illustrations of this mood are "Conversation-Starter for a Renewed Ecumenical Vision in Asia," by Preman Niles of the CCA staff, and the editorial "The Church in the Uncertainties of the Eighties," in the April 1980 *NCC Review* of India by Mathai Zachariah of the NCCI staff. That is, if we take the churches organized ecclesiastically or as local congregations of such ecclesiastical bodies, there is no appreciable movement in an ecumenical direction.

No doubt, the regional and national ecumenical councils are constituted by official churches; and their membership has grown through the years. The evolution from Western missions to independent churches had been fast within the churches and the national councils. This trend has strengthened movements of church union in Asia. Some church union moves have successfully comprised several Western confessional traditions to form new churches on a regional basis (for example, the Church of North India). There have also been developments towards full communion among different churches leading also to steps which take them towards a fuller organic-*cum*-conciliar unity (for example the CSI-CNI-Mar Thoma Joint Council). The resulting concelebrations of the eucharist and regular mutual intercession in the liturgy show a certain transcendence of East-West religious and ethnic cultural divisions which would have been impossible before the impact of ecumenism.

But these steps are also rather hesitant and halting, and it is even doubtful that they represent the ecumenical consciousness of the local congregations, which often have an ethnic rather than a Christian identity. In fact the tribal, caste, and ethnic identities of the churches and local congregations constantly threaten already established unions, prevent the implementation of schemes of union agreed to at the theological level (for example, the CSI-Lutheran union scheme), and hinder further advances towards fuller union. This is true not only in India but in other countries of Asia as well. The general impression is that the churches, understood as ecclesiastical organizations of local congregations, have had but minimum impact on *their pattern of life*.

The truth is that the ecclesiastical leadership of churches and the lay leadership of local congregations find it hard to follow the ecumenical vision of spiritual liberation from the patterns of a bygone era. These patterns have been institutionalized; and the vested interests related to them — not only social but also moral, religious, and psychological — are too strong to dislodge. As I have said, there has been substantial strengthening of regional and national ecumenical instruments of inter-church cooperation, but that may have happened because of the prestige of ecumenism and because these groups are seen as channels for Western inter-church aid and tools for defending minority communal interests *vis-à-vis* state and society — both of which are new forms of attitudes which characterized the Vasco da Gama era. Even the pressures of new Asian governments seem to strengthen the self-consciousness of the Christian community as a defensive minority searching for a way to settle down as a protected religious group rather than to be the sign of salvation for all the people of the nation and the sacrament of the divine destiny of the nation itself.

This is the danger about which Visser 't Hooft warned in 1959: "The churches which had to live in an environment dominated by other religions have become what in the Turkish empire was called a *millet* — that is more or less introverted, self-contained and isolated minority groups which did not attempt to share their faith with the majority. We must take take such historical warnings seriously, for that is what might happen to the churches in Asia." No doubt, the dominant gnostic climate of Asian societies is different from the Semitic religious climate of the Turkish empire, but the danger is no less real.

Granted, in countries like Indonesia the evangelistic emphasis of the churches may not have slackened in the post-independence period. New joint missions have been promoted by Asian churches, for instance, Nepal, but in general the Asian churches have an individualistic kind of piety, which has no awareness of the relevance of the gospel of Christ for the corporate life of the people. The Church Growth projects try to exploit the corporate groupings but have not developed any message to the ethics of the groups. Evangelical crusader and charismatic movements — some of them rooted in the West rather than in Asia — have strengthened the theology of individual pietism. Recently, however, some sections of conservative evangelicalism have moved in the direction of relating the gospel to culture and society, as a recent Madras consultation of the Evangelical Fellowship of India has evidenced, thanks to Willowbank and other consultations of the Lausanne follow-up.[2]

---

2. See *Willowbank Report on Gospel and Culture*; and see *South-East Asian Journal of Theology*, XIX, No. 2 (1978), 38ff., 50ff., for a discussion of the Report in an Asian context.

On the whole, however, the ecumenical vision of communicating the gospel of Christ to the representatives of higher traditional gnostic cultures and modern secular ideologies has not been taken up seriously by the churches. Several Christian centres for study of religions and changing society are found in Asia, and these have brought to light the underground movement to rethink Christianity in indigenous terms, which existed in the young churches of Asia even during the missionary era. They have also developed dialogues with adherents of other religions and with secular ideologies. Bishop Lakshman Wickremesurgh of Kurunagela in Sri Lanka mentions many groups in Asia which are involved in "multireligious dialogue between religious faiths" in the context of "multi-religious societies committed to nation-building." He also shows how these dialogues have given the Asian Christians involved a "fresh self-understanding of Jesus Christ and his way of salvation."[3] But surveys have shown that these have made little impact on the life-pattern of the churches as churches. This is not to deny the genuine interest church hierarchies and theological institutions have shown in new experiments in indigenous worship and evangelism and developments in Asian patterns of theology. But even they stand isolated in such matters from the life of the congregations and organized churches.

On the relation of the selfhood of the church to the nation and its people there has been no vagueness in ecumenical utterances. The EACC Assembly of 1959 made the point strongly that the selfhood of the Asian churches did not lie in preoccupation with itself, but in its concern for all the people and the whole nation. It asked it its message that the church "not become a religious ghetto, separated from Christ's mission and disobedient to his will, by becoming primarily concerned only with its own domestic affairs and organizational prosperity and growth." The message of the Sixth Assembly of the CCA said more strongly that the selfhood of Asian churches lay in their orientation to Asian people. The published collection of major statements by the EACC between 1958 and 1964 bore the title *The Christian Community within the Human Community*. The church's dialogue with the new Asia, leading to a reinterpretation of Christianity in Asian terms and to the transformation of Asian human life in Christ, is declared to be the focal point of Asian ecumenism. Nor is this conceived as a purely academic theological task but as something to be realized within the framework of dialogic ex-

---

3. *Togetherness and Uniqueness: Living Faiths in Inter-Relation*; published by the consultants to the Archbishops of Canterbury and York on Interfaith Relations (London, 1979).

istence. The church is to participate in the common struggle of the Asian people for their humanity in religion, culture, society, and state, by fighting against oppressive indigenous traditions which have been made more pathological by Western individualism and the collectivism of a technological society.

T.V. Philip is correct that church union becomes meaningful only if it is pursued as part of — or even as subsidiary to — the Asian church's search for an authentic selfhood integrally related to the struggle of the Asian people for their selfhood.[4]

It is here more than in the question of church union as such that the Asian churches have found it hard to pursue the ecumenical vision. Preman Niles says, "As it turned out, the ecumenical vision — the human community within which the Christian community would play its role — has not been realized. And the present trend seems to indicate that it may not be realizable." Perhaps. But the ecumenical vision is not that the selfhood of Asian Christianity is dependent on the realization of human community and responsible society, but that it involves the church's participation in the struggle for it with the Asian people.

Indeed, the Asian churches have found this participation with the people's struggle difficult, for the simple reason that the path to human community, or to a national community transcending linguistic, tribal, ethnic, caste, racial, and religious "communalities" has been very rough within each nation. The churches found that they themselves were historically too much a part of the divisive "communalism" to be able to transcend it and make their contribution to humanize society. Furthermore, political and economic structures in Asia were becoming too authoritarian and anti-people, so that a defense of such human rights as civil freedom and social justice involved the churches in a political stance and ministry which were too costly compared to the models of Christian service the churches were used to. Mother Teresa gets a Nobel Prize and the Bharat Ratna award, India's highest. But Archbishop Romero gets shot, and the Korean Christian poet Kim Chi Ha, who advocated people's rights and civil liberties, is jailed in a solitary cell for years by the Park regime. Naturally the churches and councils of churches hesitate to follow the poet's model to become the voice of the voiceless oppressed; instead, they continue to follow Mother Teresa's model, maintaining service institutions and even moving into development projects on a large scale. This is not to underrate the spiritual dedication, witness to Christ, and service to

---

4. "Church Unity Discussions in India," in *Ecumenism in India: Essays in Honour of M. A. Thomas*, ed. M. Zachariah (Delhi, 1980).

human beings which they evidence thereby. But one suspects that they are being used to buttress existing oppressive structures of society.

The churches have tried to say loudly that they have nothing to do with radical groups of Christians in the struggle for people's rights. The National Christian Council of India went so far as to push out of the framework of its development agency those development projects which had even a minimum programme of social transformation through people's organization and agitation. And in the Emergency the Indian churches refused even to identify themselves with a humanitarian project to aid the suffering families of the political detainees.

The record is not so dismal in all Asia. In Indonesia, the approach of the churches to the political detainees and their families was one of greater Christian solidarity. In Korea the National Council of Churches was itself involved in a costly struggle against the Park dictatorship. A good many religious orders and a sizeable section of the Roman Catholic hierarchy and congregations have been involved in resistance against the martial law regime of Marcos in the Philippines. These have been sources of renewal of the churches, in their understanding both of the gospel and of the nature of the selfhood of the Asian churches. But they are exceptions.

The general failure of the Asian churches to live up to the ecumenical vision has led T.K. Thomas to ask whether it is possible "that the churches have abdicated the ecumenical vision, that they found its demands too exacting — and too distracting — as they pursued their churchly programmes?"

The ecumenical strategy

Where does the ecumenical vision have some reality in Asia? What should be the ecumenical strategy for the development of Asian ecumenism in the 1980s?

From the beginning ecumenism has been a subversive — even an underground — movement within the churches, constituted by ecumenically committed individuals and groups. It was indeed an advance when churches officially accepted the ecumenical ideal and developed an ecclesiastical ecumenism. But today further advances in ecclesiastical ecumenism depend on the strength of the underground movement of ecumenical groups which are still the *avant-garde* of the ecumenical movement — not groups isolated and separated from the churches but groups in dialogue with the people in the congregations and with the organized churches, creating the tension and ferment of renewal. The continuing task of the ecumenical organs of the churches is to foster the ecumenically committed subversives in the churches and their dialogue with the churches.

Recently Metropolitan Paulos Mar Gregorios of the Orthodox Church of India, himself a leader of ecumenical organizations at the world and regional levels, has made the point that ecumenical pioneering and ecumenical witness are even now the responsibility of ecumenical groups within the churches, but outside their official control.[5] "It is naive to assume that the church as a whole will be faithful to the fullness of its vocation. The official church is always likely to be fulfilling some of its tasks while neglecting others, and quite often standing in the way of genuine liberation and social righteousness." In his opinion, "criticizing the church may be too lazy and unproductive." The church's vocation is to undertake a "pastoral role towards revolutionaries," to interpret socio-economic and political reality fearlessly, to exorcise the evil powers of society, to expose the ideological fetters of Christians and the "questionable character" of current economic concepts, and to support revolutionary movements or parties. But the official churches cannot do these things because they too often lack the insight or courage to challenge the establishment and are often hampered by vested interests and fear of the cross. Thus individuals and small groups within the church should undertake these responsibilities on its behalf. "The central task in praxis and theology devolves upon small groups within the Church"; and it is the "role of a proper liberation theology," which takes transcendence seriously, to be "the handmaid of this task." I presume that Mar Gregorios would extend this approach to cover other ecumenical tasks — the search for church union, dialogue with other religions, and reinterpretation of Asian Christianity, as well as the theological explorations related to them.

I suspect that the Metropolitan's thesis emerges from the practical experience of one who, as church ecclesiastic and ecumenical leader, has had to speak and act in different capacities and on different wavelengths; and it thus expresses a deeply felt truth of the church situation everywhere. But one must question his dismissal of the dialogue between the "official churches" and the "small groups" as unproductive. It looks like an apology for an inactive church and almost lets the official churches off the hook. If the small groups act in the name of the church, they must seek to bring the official church into the picture; and if the official church sees significance in what the small groups are doing it must recognize that and provide them spiritual support even if it cannot follow them. Otherwise ecclesiastical ecumenism and underground group ecumenism will be repudiating each other. Even the of-

---

5. "Main Tasks of Theology Today: Interpreting the Theology of Liberation," *NCC Review*, April 1980.

ficial church may respond in some, if not all, historical situations according to its theological convictions! With this proviso, I would agree with the Metropolitan. And the agents of the ecumenical movement should probably give priority to the development of ecumenically committed groups — of lay men and women, of clergy, of frontier groups, of radical groups — and the deepening of their ecumenical vision, praxis, and theology.

This is the strategy D.T. Niles has pursued in the East Asia Christian Conference. In his 1968 report as General Secretary of the EACC he said: "It is my hope, perhaps my illusion," that the EACC should mean a fellowship of Asian churches, "out of which there is growing a common life pursued by men and women scattered in the churches who share a common vision" and whose main task is "the creation of a group of people" who share a common ecumenical vision and are influenced by it "in the normal work they do in our churches and countries."

Should this group have its own ecumenism, parallel to the ecclesiastical ecumenism? This is in some sense inevitable. Ron O'Grady says that the Asian groups which take the ecumenical movement seriously are "those on the frontiers which struggle for the rights of the people but which do so from a lonely and vulnerable position"; they need "insights and encouragement of similar groups in other countries because their stand goes beyond nationalism to those deeper human realities of sin and suffering."[6]

The Korean leaders in the struggle against the Park regime spoke of an invisible *koinonia*, across many of the traditional barriers to fellowship, which they experienced in their suffering. Striving alongside others for human rights in Korea faced the small Christian group "with a new kind of spiritual community ... a new kind of *koinonia* which transcends the traditionally defined Christian community," in the words of Kim Kwan Suk. There was in this also "a new sense of communication" with the vast majority of silent people, Christians and otherwise, and a "sense of majority complex" resulting from solidarity with the people of God and Jesus Christ across national and ideological frontiers. "We experience the emergence of an invisible *ekklesia* which is transforming historical reality and is introducing a new history in our land." The mark of this new *ekklesia* is "continuous repentance," leading to participation in God's universal mission. This ecumenical experience of the deepest kind made them endure.[7]

---

6. Ron O'Grady, *Bread and Freedom* (Geneva, 1979).
7. See S.K. Chatterji, *The Meaning of the Indian Experience — The Emergency* (Madras, 1978), pp. 98-102.

This must also have been the experience of some of the urban-rural mission groups and the CCPD contact groups and others scattered throughout Asia, who have put the people's struggle for social transformation at the centre of their social diakonia among urban slum dwellers, rural women, and landless outcastes. As a WCC/CCA Consultation comments, "Many such fellowships in Asia are struggling in agony and silence, yet they somehow provide a pervasive sign of hope for the community of tomorrow.[8] Not only the groups for radical social change, but also clergy fellowships and theological groups committed to rethinking Christianity in Asia, fellowships committed to ecumenical evangelism, and others have the same vision of the invisible *koinonia*; it is a real if partial realization of the ecumenical vision of the *Una Sancta*. However momentary, it is what sustains them. This is what happened in the small "work groups" at the Nairobi Assembly of the World Council of Churches. It may be difficult to fit into ecclesiology, but it is there. And ecclesiastical ecumenism transcends itself and moves forward under its impact and stimulus. Here lies the hope for "the official churches" and their ecclesiastical ecumenism.

From this perspective one can second the reminder of CCA General Secretary Yap Kim Hao that CCA is a fellowship of churches and "not merely of individuals in different countries who have captured the ecumenical vision." But one has to look with suspicion at any attempt to carry this theory to the point of weakening rather than strengthening unofficial ecumenically committed groups. Ecumenism is alive today and will be alive tomorrow in the dialogue among ecumenically committed groups and in the dialogue and tension between these groups and the official churches.

8. *Ibid.*, p. 106.